Contents

I. A Talk to God

II. Self Reflection

III. Convictions

IV. Just Another Day

V. Distinction Between Consciousness & Ego

VI. Constraints of Language

Short Plays & Essays

By

Preston Iheanacho

To my brothers and sisters,

    Thank you for simply listening

I.   A Talk to God

> As Davis drudgingly walks out of the bar he is reminded that he's been here before. It's yet again another early morning/ late night for Davis as he leaves the bar in attempt to make his way home. Inebriated and flat out plastered drunk, fumbling his keys while walking, he catches himself with enough composure to keep from falling. His phone rings.

DAVIS

Hello?.....Hello?! (Beat) Hey. Yeah I know…..I know. I'm sorry I've been busy with wo-……. (Beat) Why do we have to do this? I told you I don't have anything. I'll give it when I can…..there's no need for that……it's not like you'll get any- (beat) she's my daughter too! (beat) oh God! Why do you have to be such a bitch about it? (Two beats)

Before Davis can give her chance to rebuttal he hangs up, knowing this wasn't the time to fight. He wasn't up to it, just didn't have the energy to go back and forth. He feels his phone vibrate from the back to back text messages he was receiving. He gives it a glance and turns it off.

DAVIS

Fuckin' cunt…..

In a joke of an attempt to sober up, Davis peers at himself through his rearview mirrors as if that was supposed to help the room from not spinning. He checks his side view mirrors while he fastens his seatbelt. He goes through his IPod so meticulously for someone who is obviously pretty drunk just to find the right song. The song that could describe how he felt or wanted to feel, apathy. He decides on "Big Jet Plane". He lets out a breathe of relief with a light smile and proceeds to leave the parking lot. As he is driving a lot he hears a sudden pop and his car goes careening into the barrier. Davis sees it all in slow motion. He didn't have time to react, but as he is going through it time seemed to stop.

DAVIS

SHI-

With a natural instinct, Davis turns the wheel in an effort to avoid hitting another car. He smashes into the barrier. He doesn't feel the impact, only hears what he think it would sound like. All Davis can hear is the ringing of a car alarm now. Stage fades to black.

Scene II

With the same clothes on, Davis abruptly wakes up in a state of shock. Not really from the pain of the crash, but because he didn't know what was going on. He listened to himself breathe. He could hear his heart beating faintly. Davis checks his body to see if he's hurt at all. He looks around in an attempt to see if he can find his car. He is astounded to realize that moment that he is nowhere near the highway. He starts to explore the new surroundings he's awakening in.

DAVIS

What the hell….Where am I?

(Spotlight turns on)

GOD

You're where you've always been…with me.

>Davis shades his eyes with his hands and looks into the bright spotlight.

DAVIS

And who the fuck are you?

GOD

Loneliness. Boredom….your father…mother…and everyone else you've known.

DAVIS

Uhh yeah…I only got one dad. Really though. What's…What's going on?

GOD

Is that a fact to you? (Beat) He left you when you were 9. Remember that? And I brought him back to you.

>Davis stood there startled, wondering who could know such facts about him. He reminisces about trying to conceal how happy he was when his dad decided to move back in when he 12.

                    DAVIS

Is this....I just left the bar right?

>   In a state of disbelief Davis paces frantically across the stage. Unwilling to accept what he felt was inevitable, he started mumbling underneath his breathe.

                    DAVIS

No....no no no no no nononono!

>   Davis stood there, feet planted, for what felt like an eternity. He held himself on the verge of crying, but couldn't bring tears to cry for himself. A young girl who he previously didn't notice grabbed his hand

                    GOD

Come on

>   She startled him, but he didn't show it. He was too exhausted to put up a fight. She led him to a table. Davis scanned his new surroundings. A game of chess was already set up. Stage lights dim on table. He

> noticed the young girl was quite interested in the next move. He didn't know if she expected him to play or if they already had been playing. He didn't care. He watched her pick up a piece and move it. Before she could finish placing it down he pushes her hand inadvertently knocking other pieces over.

DAVIS

Can you help me? I mean I can't today! Please…..I can't. Please (beat) I told my mom I was going to stop by and yeah! My brother's game! I can't and Paige….I can't do this to her. I can't I can't I can't.

> Davis briskly tries to walk off stage only to find out there is nowhere for him to go. The young girl watches him struggle and panic to find and exit yet doesn't change her demeanor the whole time.

GOD

Something's even I can't change….that I'm truly sorry for. You're at the point of eternal bliss and few get in. Now please… your time to speak. Let me know why you should be let in.

> Somewhat half heartedly, Davis admits defeat in his body

language. He abruptly tries to maintain some composure and threads of dignity left remaining. He finds himself wiping off tears he didn't even know were there.

DAVIS

(Pause) Well I'm not gonna sit here and tell you I'm a devout Christian or big on any religion or that I even attempted to read the bible…..but I don't think I've done too much wrong my entire time living. Never killed anyone…ever. Never tried to either.

(Long Dead Silence)

DAVIS

And I've always…always tried to be a good person. I mean…even when I was suicidal at one point…I I got through it. Been a caretaker my whole life too (two beats) Even when I've been burned. Shit only you know how many times I've still tried to help people.

GOD

You stole from your mother's purse.

DAVIS

I was fuckin' 10!

GOD

It's still a sin.

> Davis crosses his arms and gives the young girl a look of resentment. Watching her stare intently at the board.

DAVIS

And yeah…I really don't understand why I have to tell you all this of you know already.

GOD

I've seen you rob people, I've seen you stea//-

DAVIS

Yeah and you made me see jail for it too if you don't remember.

GOD

I've seen you lay your hands on a female. Sold drugs to parents…none of that was needed my son.

DAVIS

(Without a drop of remorse in his voice)

I'm……..I don't know what to say. I'm sorry for that. I really am.

> Davis looks down at his feet in an ashamed manner, the same look a young boy would have when talking to disappointed parents

GOD

Are you sorry for abandoning your child? Cheating on every girl you've been with? Doing wrong to people that have only wanted the best for you?

> Davis immediately looks up at the young girl, almost taken aback. Davis had no rationalization for getting defensive. It just felt better. Felt safer.

DAVIS

Really? We're going there? First off, when it comes to baby momma's god....YOU gave me the worst fuckin' one.

> The young girl continues to place the chess pieces back in their designated place, she doesn't even look Davis in the eye

GOD

That was your second child (beat) you shouldn't have killed the first one.

> Anger begin to show in Davis' face.

DAVIS

Really? Really?! I was 17…..17 with no job…no fuckin' pot to piss in and you wanted me to bring a child into the world I couldn't take care of? What sort of parent are you?

> The girl moves a piece and sits back in her chair finally meeting eyes with Davis.

GOD

Your move

> Davis still unwilling to play the game with the girl simply glares at her. She waits for him, but he doesn't move. She lets out a sigh and grabs the board and moves a piece for him.

GOD

I gave you a blessing and you made the wrong decision.

DAVIS

Maybe so…I mean but who hasn't. I've done alotta things I'm not proud of…..I'm sure you have too.

> Reluctantly and slowly, Davis caves and moves a piece on the table. He is surprised to look up and see the young girl lightly smiling at him.

DAVIS

Look I'm not here to beg….just please.

GOD

You're made in my image but you've held on to resentments...even in doing business. The discord. I tell you to lead by example (beat) to teach forgiveness and you never do.

> Davis looks at the girl, wanting to retort but decides against it.

GOD

You lived with anger (beat) envy, (beat) greed, (beat) pride, (beat) sloth, lust even gluttony. You know as well as I what you've felt. What you've done.

DAVIS

I'm not going to sit here and tell you anything different than you're telling me. I'm not perfect...I'm human.....Too fuckin'human....I'm fickle. I'm just like you.

GOD

That I do understand. Even so, when I take you out of trouble's way you don't think to.....Should every time I hear from you be you asking what I could do for you? I've blessed you with family, health, and wealth...All those blessing. You still ask for help.

> The acerbity of the situation begins to perturb Davis to an extent where he feels attacked by the accusations. Davis begins to retort in a heated fashion.

DAVIS

Ok (beat) I'll admit….there's been times in my life I needed help to do things. To make money. And I've done something's I'm not proud of. I got a question for you though….Why everything I loved you managed to take from me?

(Long Silence)

> Enraged and brooding with resentment that God doesn't reply DAVIS' voice begins to rise

DAVIS

You stand there acting perfect and shit and question a motherfucker who tries…I really try! I even found ways when you kept dealing fucked up ass cards.

> The young girl stares blankly. Now Davis' voice can't hide his anger and he begins yelling

DAVIS

You make mistakes like me as far as I can see! Rich people win the lottery…You give us war, cancer and greed…You even let skinny people starve and give obese fuckers food! Fuck you. Don 't stand there like it's all ok.

> Davis gets up from the table. Looks at the girl

DAVIS

Don't fuckin sit there and tell me I'm fuckin up...I mean the nerve ...The fuckin audacity of you to tell me I'm wrong. That you....That you picked my time like that...Aids drugs and guns? Oh it's cool for them to stay huh?

GOD

Anything else you'd take for granted//

DAVIS

Take a fuckin look at yourself before you call me out. You're...your fuckin' cold hearted.....What type of maker brings babies into the world retarded? What type of sick son of a bitch do you have to be to do something like that?

GOD

Who do you take me for? (beat) I can't do anything for you that you can't do for yourself///

DAVIS

No no no no no... fuck you fuck that. I truly don't give a shit anymore. I mean really. I've done what I've had to for ME to survive! I sinned because I was in hell. No gates..no bliss...just hardships, failure and loss....The worst part of it all..of everything was the continuous search for how I'd find the strength tomorrow to go on doing what I did today. For what I've been doing. Running around for these stupid ass people, these stupid ass projects. Everything. It comes to nothing. Each meager attempt only to help forget the dread of more and more insecure tomorrows//

GOD

You speak so matter of factly. Do you really want happiness? Actual happiness always looks pretty, how would I put this? Unfit, in comparison with the overcompensations of misery. Stability isn't nearly as spectacular as instability. Being contented has none of the glamour as a good fight against misfortune (beat) none of the picturesqueness of a struggle with temptation, or a fatal overthrow by passion....or doubt. Happiness is never grand. Happiness is for fools.

DAVIS

> He puts his elbows on the table and rests his face in his hands.

DAVIS

I must be a fool then. I'm done. What's the reason for my hardships?...Can you tell me now? I'm already fucking dead

GOD

Do you really want to know?

DAVIS

Yes! I Do !

GOD

To be a better man than you were yesterday. Life has no meaning. Each of us has meaning and we bring it to life. It is a waste to be asking the question when you are the answer.

Immediately as GOD spoke these words DAVIS wakes up still strapped into the seat of a wrecked car.

Play Ends

II. Self- Reflection

It's around 5:56 AM and Adam tries to get out of bed as quietly as possible in an attempt to not wake the girl who happens to be sleeping right next to him. Adam proceeds to walk to the living room and scans the dimly light room. To his surprise, he finds a few party favors from the night before left amidst. Hungry and hungover, Adam, in a midst of apathy goes over and to eats the chocolate covered mushrooms and eyes the leftover cocaine residue on the living room counter. He walks up to the counter and rubs the leftover amount on his gums. While walking through the living room back to his bedroom Adam quietly steps over bodies of friends and acquaintances he made the previous night. All the details of a 'fun' night lay amidst the cluttered living room. Sleeping women, alcohol bottles, cigarette butts, and an empty Ziploc bag that contained a quarter of cocaine is crumbled up underneath a girl he was sure to meet in the coming morning hours. He walks back to the restroom leans over the sink and begins washing his face hastily. He then lights a cigarette and continues to look at himself in the mirror. To his surprise Adam's reflection doesn't pick up a cigarette.

ADAM

That can't be right....hmmm?

Adam slowly begins doing gestures hoping his reflection does the same. His reflection then begins mimicking his gestures, after a few seconds his reflection bursts out in laughter.

ADAM'S REFLECTION

Hahaha alright alright I can't do this anymore....the look on your face was priceless.

ADAM

I'm sorry I'm still. It's just. I mean I'm talking to myself...I don't know if this is the mushrooms or me or both or I don't know. I do know I'm too high too panic.

> Adam ashes his cigarette on the sink and peers curiously and inquisitively into the mirror.

ADAM

I have a cigarette in my hand and you do//

ADAM'S REFLECTION

Yeah I don't smoke. Well you do...I don't. I quit a while back...remember that time when you tried to inhale a cigar? I thiiiiink I felt that one worse than you did.

ADAM

And you can't be me...I'm white and//

ADAM'S REFLECTION

Lactose intolerant?

ADAM

(Adam points at the mirror while talking)

No smart ass...I'm white and well...you're your black.

> Adam's reflection looks down at himself then raises up his arms to search his body as if he had a blemish on himself.

ADAM'S REFLECTION

Black? What does that mean? I'm you...I've always been you. Throughout life when I look into the mirror or when you do, you're what I see.

> Adam briskly walks to the bedroom and searches for a small mirror, he eyes one grabs it and hurries back to the restroom and puts it up to the mirror so his reflection can see himself.

ADAM

I don't see you. See...You don't look like me.

> Adam's reflection gazes into the mirror and a smirk begins to develop on his reflection's face

ADAM'S REFLECTION

Wow...your right. I'm prettier. And a bit funnier I might say....Nah really though I have to be you. I've always been around....kinda like the Verizon guy except less creepy.

ADAM

Dude you're not me...has to be the drugs. If I was you I couldn't be me.

ADAM'S REFLECTION

If you're not me than I'm not me and then who am I?....I mean I am in a mirror. I think it's safe to say we're the same person wouldn't you?

ADAM

Can't be...

ADAM'S REFLECTION

Well how about you figure out who you are...

ADAM

I'm Adam Kostas. The real one.

ADAM'S REFLECTION

Sure about that? Because obviously me too....are you Adam? Or you just stating the internalized supposition based on what everyone's told you.

> Adam pauses for a second in an attempt to gather his words

ADAM

I'm Adam ...I...I have to be. Grew up on Lancaster Dr. I got two brothers and a sister.

ADAM'S REFLECTION

Ah yes the futile memories of a nonexistent childhood. This should be fun. Let's tart from the beginning...Who are you? What are you?

ADAM

Well first off I'm a man. I'm a human. That's about it right? I mean I'm me...my personality my thoughts.

> Adam points at his chest.

ADAM'S REFLECTION

What is personality anyway, something Alzheimer's can take away? Preferences, experiences, opinions....a ball of clay? Whoa.....Who's that?

> Adam's reflection cranes his neck over Adam to peer into the bedroom. Adam turns around to see who he is talking about.

ADAM

Who Ashley?

ADAM'S REFLECTION

That's the one from the tailgate?!.... Wait wasn't she a freshman?

ADAM

Hey if there's grass on the field...play ball.

                    ADAM/ADAM'S REFLECTION
(Simultaneously)

And if there is no grass turn around and play in the mud.

                                        Both of them let out a
                                        light laught. Adam
                                        lights another cigarette

                    ADAM'S REFLECTION

Wait...Where's Monica? Isn't she coming today?

                            ADAM

Fuck! I almost forgot. She said she should be here by early afternoon I think.

                                        Adam walks over to his
                                        phone to check his text
                                        messages from Monica
                                        to confirm her arrival
                                        time. A vacuous smile
                                        forms on Adam's face
                                        as he reads her text
                                        messages. Adam puts
                                        the phone back down
                                        and returns the
                                        restroom.

                            ADAM

I gotta tell her...I can't.

                        ADAM'S REFLECTION

Can't what? What the hell are you talkin about?

                ADAM

Monica….It's just that…everything. I need to tell her the truth.

                ADAM'S REFLECTION

Whoa whoa whoa slow down there Ricky Bobby. Who said you can't have your cake and eat it too?

                ADAM

Dude…she's coming today and the last time we've seen each other was 4 months ago. She doesn't even know I smoke! I feel like everything's changed.

                ADAM'S REFLECTION

Before you go crying to her how you've changed how about you figure out who you are first….

> Suddenly, Adam's phone rings. He goes to the bed and reaches over a sleeping Ashley to grab it. His eyes widen as he realizes it's a text from Monica. He hurriedly walks back to the restroom.

                ADAM

What and how do I respond to this? And what do you mean? I do know who I am. You don't know who you are….you're the black guy.

ADAM'S REFLECTION

Firstly...I'm brown and what does that have to do with anything? I'm still you

ADAM

You're not. Just how I know I'm white you have to know that. This side of the mirror that matters.

ADAM'S REFLECTION

It's never stopped me before

ADAM

Its' because you obviously live in a mirror, and if you didn't know any better it's about to...see there's certain places society will only let you get to...for you that'll be athlete entertainer or a criminal.

ADAM'S REFLECTION

Wait what?

ADAM

Pretty much everything from portrayal in the media to the application of state authority to even treatment in the criminal justice system is based on who or "what" you are. Education, health care even housing...That's why you have to know.

ADAM'S REFLECTION

I don't want to be any of those things.... I write...and dude I grew up with you... why are you even talking like that? I've never experienced this subliminal intolerance you seem to be so aware of.

ADAM

If you REALLY are my reflection and you've seen this world I don't see how you can't see it.

ADAM'S REFLECTION

Why do I have to? Seems unnecessary

ADAM

Just the way it is.

ADAM'S REFLECTION

No it's not. That's a cop out. Call me naïve but I don't... What it seems like to me is that YOU and the rest of these "supposed" people you speak of have this insecurity and inferiority complex more than I do....and I'm the brown one. For anybody to use race to affirm their own identity seems pretty insecure

ADAM

Yeah it's unfortunate...just the way it is.

ADAM'S REFLECTION

Again. I hear what you're saying but I don't think like that. I never associated with this so called being "black" or whatever I'm supposed to be....kinda just grew up loving the life experience...It's hard to even call myself human.

ADAM

What do you mean by that?

> Adam's reflection leans in towards the mirror and looks Adam directly in the eye

ADAM'S REFLECTION

Have you ever felt that your real soul was invisible to your mental vision and the reality we live in...except...except in a few hallowed moments?

ADAM

Nah...but talking like that I would definitely lay off the drugs if I was you.

ADAM'S REFLECTION

Ok Charlie Sheen. I just saw you licking the counter over there to get a buzz//

ADAM

You saw that? And just sayin' that's that crazy man talk.

ADAM'S REFLECTION

No I mean...I don't know. (Beat) I just think that being human is weird. I think we ....Well I just don't really think any of this is real or even matters. I kind of think these human vessels or just that...vessels. I don't want to get too attached to something that is temporary....especially since we have little to no control of choosing these vessels. The experience for me anyways is all that matters and the imprint we leave on others...Only thing I wanna do is do right. That makes me feel good. Life is a feeling process.

> Adam pauses for a second and begins feeling a twinge of guilt for his questionable state of affairs with Monica.

> ADAM

Yeah I gotta tell her.

> Adam grabs his phone and sends Monica the cliché "we need to talk" text messages. As soon as he presses send Adam's heart drops in regret of sending that message. Adam suddenly walks directly to the mirror and begins chastising his reflection.

> ADAM

Shit I shouldn't have done that. Why did you let me send that? This is your fault!

> Adam points his finger directly in his reflection's face. To Adam's surprise, his reflection goes through the mirror and grabs Adam's outstretched finger and begins to twist it. Adam lets out a quiet yelp of pain trying to not wake up the others in the house.

ADAM

Oww! Oww! I'm sorry I'm sorry! //

ADAM'S REFLECTION

//First off, don't put your hand in my face. Secondly, I didn't tell you to send the message. I didn't even tell you what to put in it......Sorry about the finger. I got a little heated.

> Adam's reflection releases Adam's finger. Adam quickly pulls in his hand, still in awe that his reflection went through the mirror.

ADAM'S REFLECTION

I get why you did it though...always helps to be truthful...I think anyways.

> Adam feels his phone vibrate. Immediately looking at it he gets the worst feeling ever.

ADAM

It's Monica...she just asked "Are you going to break up with me?" What do I say? What do I say? I don't want to hurt her.

ADAM'S REFLECTION

Damn...Yeah I'm not Dr.Phil but just text her and ask her would she still want to be with you if she found out you cheated on her.

ADAM

Better to be honest right?

> Adam sends Monica the text messages awaiting Monica's reply as if it was an impending court sentence. Suddenly Adam hears a rustling sound coming from the bed and footsteps outside the door.

ASHLEY

Baby you O.K in there?

ADAM

(Mumbling underneath his breath)

Shit…. how do I get her out of here before Monica comes?

ADAM'S REFLECTION

Don't ask me…I'm just your reflection.

> Adam's reflection walks backwards until he is out of sight.

ADAM

(Underneath his breath)

No help you are asshole….

ASHLEY

Hey you ok? Sounds loud in there.

ADAM

(Speaking through the door)

Yeah yeah...just getting ready for work.

ASHLEY

Aww I didn't know you worked today. There's some food from yesterday. Let me make you some breakfast before you go!

Ashley swiftly gets out of bed and runs to the kitchen. While she is out of the room Adam pokes his head out the door and finally comes out of the restroom when he finds out he has the room to himself.

ADAM

(To himself)

Yeah I'll just tell everybody that I gotta go to work then come back here and clean up before Monica gets here.

Adam looks at his phone awaiting a text message from Monica

> but she still hasn't replied. This is a little surprising to Adam as for the whole time he's been dating Monica she always replied relatively fast

ADAM

(To himself)

36 texts a day…that's 252 texts a week. 52 weeks in the year…that's like 13,000 texts a year. 4 years in it wow.

> Adam eyes glaze over as he reminisces past experiences in his and Monica's relationship. He is woken out of the day dream by the smell of pizza and Chinese food. Ashley walks back into the room and sits on the bed with two plates filled with food.

ASHLEY

It's a bit of a concoction, but hopefully it helps you have a good day at work.

> Ashley leans in and kisses Adam on the cheek.

ASHLEY

Imma turn on the TV babe.

> Ashley walks to the TV and turns it on. As she flips through the channels she stops on Channel 9 Fox news. Ashley sits down next to Adam on the bed. After a couple bites into the meal Adam drops and breaks his plate leaving his food all over the floor.

ADAM

This can't be happening

ASHLEY

What's wrong?

> Adam over hears the rush hour news report about an accident that blocked off Interstate-10 caused by a blue Honda Civic.

ADAM

Monica drives a blue Honda Civic…..

Adam looks down at his phone one more time still awaiting a reply.

Play Ends

III. Convictions

Nurses, doctors, and janitors all walk it seems in slow motion as Luke sits on a bench in the hospital. Luke is looking at the floor tapping his foot at a faster pace than the people that are walking across him in the hospital. Suddenly a doctor comes up to Luke and everything goes back to real time.

DOCTOR

Excuse me….. Luke correct?

LUKE

Yeah yeah I'm her brother.

                    (Long pause)

                              The people walking
                              across in the hospital
                              slowdown from real
                              time showing the angst
                              and wait Luke feels
                              while awaiting a reply
                              from the Doctor. The
                              doctor puts his hand
                              out for a handshake

                    DOCTOR

I'm Dr. Adams...we have managed to stabilize Sarah.

                    LUKE

That's good. Is she gonna be ok?

                    DOCTOR

She….There's some damage and she hasn't gained full control of all her bodily functions.

                    LUKE

What? What do you mean? Y'all stabilized her I thought?

                    DOCTOR

We've stabilized her in the sense that she's alive…..During the accident she was hit from behind and sustained trauma to her skull and spinal region.

LUKE

Is she gonna be ok? Can I see her?

DOCTOR

We're doing the best we can. She isn't allowed visitors at the moment but we're hoping that she can improve within the next 48 hours in order for family to be able to visit. Get some rest yourself. In the next couple of days you and the rest of your family can come and visit her.

LUKE

In her only family......Just me for now.

DOCTOR

Well I can contact you and let you know when we see any change. In the meantime get some rest. She'll need you at your best when she comes to.

> Doctor Adams walks away briskly. The sound of his footsteps can be heard very loudly. Luke stands there as many nurses doctors and employees pass by Luke in real time.

Scene fades to black

Scene 2

> Young man dressed in a suit sits on the corner of the stage

smoking a cigarette. Spotlight turns on.

ALEX

Some people say life is a game of chess...I think it's a game of poker. Ya always gotta deal with what cards are given. Ya know? and ya never know what anyone else has in their hands. Hell sometimes life forces ya to play a hand you wouldn't want to play. And well today....well today is just one of those days.

Alex hears a loud knock on the other end of the stage he abruptly gets up to answer the door. 2 men soaking wet all dressed up in suits come in holding newspapers and a couple of umbrellas over their head trying their best to stay dry in the midst of a thunderstorm.

ALEX

Took ya fuckin long enough……

DERRICK

We got caught up behind the train. It literally took forever. We're still on schedule though right?

ALEX

Yeah...where's Luke?

ANDREW

I brought everything you asked...it's all in there//

ALEX

//Where's Luke?

DERRICK

He said he'll meet us up here. He had something's to take care of.

ALEX

The fuck is that mean? It's a 3 man job. That's why I kept saying make sure you all come together //

> Just as Alex was chastising Derrick a knock is heard at the door. Derrick goes to and answers it, Luke walks in.

LUKE

Sorry I'm late, I had some family things to take care of.

DERRICK

No worries. We're all here now.

ALEX

Ok, well let's make sure we do this right.

> Alex picks up rolled up paper and puts the layout of the house on a table. The three men gather around the table.

ALEX

We enter through here. Remember....once were in I need you two to immediately to go to the back.

DERRICK

Sounds like a plan.

ALEX

Luke... you and me are responsible for watch in front and the safe. We have literally 3 minutes tops to get in and out. No games. We've practiced this before fellas this should be like taking candy from a baby.

LUKE

I'm sorry I just I don't know. I'm not too sure about this. Something just feels off. I mean we only scoped it out for a few weeks

> Alex walks over to Luke and gets in his face.

ALEX

God damn don't bitch up on me now. I need the money he needs the money and you need the money....Simple as that. If you don't want your cut just let me know. I'm sure no one here would mind taking it.

LUKE

I'm not saying that. I'm just saying something doesn't feel right. Maybe it's the weather. I'm not bitching out or anything…..Fuck it lets just get it over with.

> Alex pulls out 3 glocks and a shotgun and hands them to each one if his counterparts.

DERRICK

Why are they loaded? Just for show remember?//

ALEX

 They are…Just thought it'd be safer to have it than not to have it…ya' know? Just making sure that baby gives us our candy. Couple shots in the air and it'll be a cakewalk.

Scene fades to black

> Spotlight turns on. Luke walks to the middle of the stage ski mask halfway on as if he's getting a breather. He is walking in a manner that shows frustration.

LUKE

I always regret it when it's too late. I wonder sometimes if I'm ever the only one this unlucky.

> Luke walks back into the scene and it begins. Moment is tense. Alex and Luke seem to look as if they worked out in their suits. Ski masks halfway off they find themselves in the bedroom. A woman is tied up and gagged in the middle of the room. She seems to be quietly sobbing.

JOANNE

I promise...I swear I won't say//

ALEX

(Yelling as he walks toward the tied up woman)

//SHUT THE FUCK UP!

LUKE

Bro let's go! Finish the safe and let's get the fuck out. You're trippin' hard.

ALEX

Did you not just see what happened? Are you stupid as fuck or what? THE BITCH SAW OUR FACE. We're fucked//

LUKE

//We're not fucked. She just said she's not going to say anything-

ALEX

You really believe this bitch? You think when we leave she isn't gonna fuckin flip on us? THE BITCH SAW MY FACE....look we're gonna have to figure this out some way.

LUKE

I don't know man...this is new. We gotta trust somebody

ALEX

You're a stupid mother fucker. Trust the bitch that's tied up that was yelling hysterically when we got in here? That's your plan?//

LUKE

We're here...YOU picked today...this is something that YOU should've been taken into account. Don't take it out on the woman because of your fuckin' mistakes.

ALEX

Don't fuckin sit there and blame this shit on me! The bitch forgot her purse. How the fuck do you account for that?//

JOANNE

ALEX I SWEAR TO GOD I WON'T SAY A THING! //

ALEX

SHE KNOWS MY NAME?!

> Luke walks up and grabs Alex by the shoulder.

LUKE

Look man....we give her some cash to shut her up. If we go down she's an accomplice. It's a win win and no one gets hurt. Trust me. We're in too deep to fuck up anything else up. Let's just go back and meet up. It's 12 minutes over. They're probably shitting bricks.

ALEX

You're right. You're right. Sorry. You're right. All this shit just has me paranoid

> Luke looks over at the tied up woman. She slums her shoulders in a relieved fashion.

LUKE

You're not going to say anything are you?

JOANNE

(Sobbing hysterically)

I swear...No. I swear I won't. I just want to go home. I got a family. I just want to go home. Please...please just let me go home.

LUKE

We have nothing to worry about. Let's just get out of here.

ALEX

You're right man. Call 'em and let em know it's a green light ok? I'll untie her.

LUKE

Sounds like a plan. I'm on it.

ALEX

> Luke walks away fumbling with his cell phone. A conversation between Luke and Andrew could be heard as he walks offstage. Leaving just Alex and a tied up and crying Joanne left in the room.

JOANNE

(Talking through tears)

Thank you so much...I swear I just want to home//

ALEX

Shut the fuck up...please.

> Alex roughly grabs the woman and escorts her SR. Once they are offstage, Luke returns

                                    from his conversation
                                    with Andrew.

                        LUKE

Aye I just called him. Their...Alex? Alex?

                                    A loud gunshot could
                                    be heard.

                        LUKE

ALEX!

                                    Alex walks back
                                    onstage. It's done. Let's
                                    get out of here.

                        LUKE

What did you do?!

                        ALEX

What you couldn't do. Let's get out of here.

                        LUKE

Where is she?

(Long Pause)

                        LUKE

Why man?! You sick son of a bitch you didn't have to.

                        ALEX

Oh I definitely did....What part of she saw our face Luke do you not get?! How fuckin stupid could you be? We got the money. We got rid of the witness. Let's clean up this fuckin place and let's get the fuck out here. Take your money save your sister and never remember today fuckin happened. That's literally all you have to do.

> Alex begins wiping the floor in an attempt to clean the area of their fingerprints.

LUKE

I never signed up for this.

ALEX

Me neither...but we're here. Now grab a cloth and start wiping.

> While Alex is picking things up from the ground, Unbeknown to Alex, Luke steps up behind him and puts a gun to the back of his head. Once the scene fades black a gunshot can be heard.

SCENE 3

> It's a Saturday afternoon and Luke timidly walks into a church. He catches himself staring at the large cross that is the most decorous piece of memorabilia in the dimly lit church. He walks over and enters a small closet-like room towards the back of the church. Luke gets on both knees and begins his confessional with the priest on the other side of the screen.

LUKE

(As he makes the cross sign)

Bless me, Father, for I have sinned…..It has been a long time since my last confession.

PRIEST

What troubles you my child?

LUKE

Since my last confession I haven't been the best I could be….I've abused drugs. I've given into temptation. I cheated on girls. I stole candy from the grocery store. I almost killed my sister. I mess with Texas and litter sometimes//

PRIEST

What…You tried to kill your sister?

LUKE

Oh that one….Yeah I feel like I should've done something to stop her from driving under the influence so it's my fault.

PRIEST

As much as we try, we cannot dictate another's actions. Each choice someone makes that person has to be responsible for.

LUKE

I've also had impure thoughts and….done some things.

PRIEST

What do you mean my child?

LUKE

I don't know if what I done was what I should've done. I don't feel any better. I thought hurting someone…hurting someone who hurt someone else would make me feel better about the things I've done. It doesn't. I was so deranged and delusional…I thought I was committing a good act.

PRIEST

What is it that you should've done?

LUKE

Forgive my father...I've sinned against someone I...an acquaintance.

PRIEST

Has he sinned against you?

LUKE

He sinned against...against someone else.

PRIEST

God only asks that you love. Even when others who have sinned against you. Love them.

> Luke begins to weep. He puts his head down and continues dialogue with the priest.

LUKE

Everything I've done was for my sister. To give life. To save her life. I've just taken life. I don't know how it all ended up like this.

PRIEST

Sometimes god's way isn't always the way we intended.

LUKE

I just don't know what way I'm supposed to go. I don't know...is it worth it? I had good intentions.

PRIEST

There are some questions I can't answer for you. All the answers you seek you already know. God resides within you.

LUKE

Yes, father. I have to confess more. My sister. The car wreck. By the time the paramedics arrived....their telling me she might never be the same. Life as a vegetable basically is her best alternative....

PRIEST

Is this a permanent situation?

LUKE

They haven't given me a definite answer...but it may be.

PRIEST

I send my condolences.

(Beat)

PRIEST

Where does your sin come into the factor?

LUKE

I don't know if it's right for her to live that way or if it's God's will.

PRIEST

God has blessed us with the capacity of forgiveness and the intellect to know better which should lead us to do better. You have not sinned my child. You're just misguided.

> Luke toils with her rosary in his hands while listening to the priest.

LUKE

You don't grant birthday wishes, do you?

PRIEST

I'm a Priest, not a genie.

LUKE

Well, the next time you talk to Him, would you ask him what he would do?

PRIEST

That I will. Through the ministry of the church may god give you pardon and peace and I absolve of your sins. In the name of the father, son and Holy Spirit…. (Two beats)That is it Luke. (Beat) There are other's waiting.

LUKE

My uncle always told me, your home isn't your home if there's an enemy there. It doesn't matter of you toss a drop cloth over it, or you decide to completely redecorate the place. Until you figure out a way to make that feeling leave, you'll never feel safe. Imagine that feeling….that feeling comes over to your house. It sits down in the living room, and no matter what...no matter what you do it won't go away. Day after day it refuses to leave. What do you do? You begin to ignore it. You pretend it's not there.

PRIEST

I'd call the police

LUKE

Just stay with me please.

PRIEST

All right all right….What's truly bothering you?

LUKE

I killed somebody…..I killed somebody. I shot a guy who I did a job with. He murdered a woman. I was hoping God could absolve me. I don't want my soul to burn in hell.

> The priest opens up the window in the confession booth and looks Luke in the eye.

PRIEST

Luke….either you're a person wondering if you have a soul, or you're a soul who knows that being a person isn't real. We're human…we're fallible…we're jealous…we laugh. Don't get frustrated. God forgives all. Remember that. No sin is too big for God's forgiveness.

> The priest gets up from his chair and walks offstage

>   leaving Luke alone in the
>   confession booth.
>
>   LUKE
>
>   (To Audience)

I really hope so.

>   Luke gets up and walks
>   offstage

Scene 4

>   Luke is sleeping
>   uncomfortably in a
>   chair at the hospital
>   with a jacket over him
>   as he tries to get some
>   rest. Sarah gets up
>   from the hospital bed
>   and attempts to try and
>   wake Luke up.
>
>   SARAH
>
>   (Softly whispering)

Luke...hey...Hey Luke.

>   Luke slowly wakes up
>   and is startled to see
>   his sister moving about.
>
>   LUKE

Sarah! Oh god! You're ok!

Luke gets up and embraces his sister with a suffocating hug.

                              SARAH

Well technically...I'm still here. Just not in there.

>   Sarah points to the hospital
>   bed where her body lies. Luke
>   looks over then back to his
>   sister. He is obviously confused
>   in what is taking place.

                              SARAH

Don't get freaked out...You're not crazy. I just had to talk to you.

>   Luke still seems pretty startled.
>   He wants to ask questions but
>   is so astounded by what's
>   taking place he can barely put
>   his words together.

                              SARAH

I'm sorry I couldn't reach you any other way. I literally jumped out of my body to tell you...well I just wanted you to know you don't have to worry about me. Just don't be afraid.

                              LUKE

I'm not worried Sarah. I swear I'm going to keep you in the best care//

                              SARAH

I mean I don't want you to be afraid of me not being here. I'm O.K.

LUKE

What do you mean? I swear. I know things aren't perfect. I'm sorry for not being there all that time. It's my fault-

SARAH

Hey don't say that//

LUKE

It is though.

SARAH

Nothing's your fault...everything happens how it's supposed to happen. Heck that night I want you to know it was my decision to get behind the wheel. It wasn't you driving.

LUKE

I just wish...

SARAH

I wish a lot of things but hey I'm not a genie and neither are you.

LUKE

A lot of people have been telling me that lately. I can't wait to meet one.

SARAH

Still as smart and clever as I left you I see.

> Sarah walks over to Luke and grabs his hand.

SARAH

You're my brother. I love you. You've always tried to look after me. Even when I didn't want you to.

> Luke looks down at the ground

LUKE

That's what I'm supposed to do. If I don't who will.

> Sarah smiles and lets out a light laugh.

SARAH

I'm O.K.....trust me. I don't want to be here forever....I'm not meant to be. I appreciate everything you've done for me so far...now....all I need you to do know is just let me go.

LUKE

I'm your brother...I'm not going to let you die. I can't...There's still a chance. I can't let you die.

SARAH

Even so...it won't be how I remembered it. It won't be the life I lived. It can't...It will never be.

> Luke looks at Sarah kind of confused because he is unsure

is she is serious about her topic.

       LUKE

Death Sarah?....Is that really what you want?

       SARAH

The music doesn't stop playing just because somebody can't hear it. Just life on another frequency.

       LUKE

I can't....I can't Sarah.

       Luke walks away from where Sarah was standing

       LUKE

I'm sorry...I can't. I'm afraid so much. I don't want to lose you. Who else I mean you're all I got.

       SARAH

Luke...The one thing I learned through this whole experience is that nothing is as unreliable as fear, and yet I kept relying on it over and over again. When this happened you don't think I was afraid? When the accident happened? When I became aware that I couldn't move any of my extremities. It was the scariest moment of my life. I was engulfed in fear.

       LUKE

What'd you do?

SARAH

I learned...learned there's nothing to be afraid of...nothing to be afraid to lose....nothing to hold onto. I had to realize what I wanted to hold onto is always going to be there.

LUKE

What the fuck are you talkin about?

SARAH

You remember that time with Mom? When we both got lost in the mall? We we're fighting over that remote controlled car...and when we turned around she wasn't there?

LUKE

Yeah I DO... I was 7...and you were 5

SARAH

I was so scared

LUKE

We both were I started shaking.

SARAH

I started to cry....I was so afraid. It didn't even matter we were fighting over the controller ...You dropped it and grabbed me and told me it was gonna be O.K..... I knew at that moment that you were always going to be by my side. I knew you loved me. (Beat) It was O.K. Mom found us. It was always O.K.

LUKE

I don't know where you're going with this-

SARAH

I mean….She was in the store the whole time. We had no reason to be afraid. She was there then as she is now.

LUKE

Mom's dead.

SARAH

Doesn't' mean she's not here.

LUKE

This is too much right now Sarah…I can't.

SARAH

Don't be afraid of fear…fear is the biggest liar. Fear tells you that you're not safe…but you are. Thinking that you aren't safe is an illusion; you're buying into the lie.

LUKE

If mom was here//

SARAH

//You're going to try to tell me all the reasons I'm wrong. Try to think if why I might be right. It took me losing my body to realize that while fear is trying to convince you that it's real, what's really happening is that you lose touch with the present…and that's what I've done.

SARAH

I'll always be here. Trust me....just like everyone else...I'll always be here.

> Luke takes a look at Sarah then walks away

LUKE

Is this really what you want?

Long Pause

SARAH

I don't have much time.... Just stop resisting for a second...I'm trying to get you to look inside yourself//

LUKE

I just have to tell you I'm sorry.

> Sarah smiles at Luke

SARAH

Death means never having to say you're sorry.

> Sarah climbs back into bed just as Doctor Adams walks into the room.

DOCTOR

Is everything o.k? Thought we heard some noise.

> Luke still emotional from his encounter

with Sarah replies to Dr. Adams.

LUKE

No it's fine. I was just talking to myself

DOCTOR

(Smiling at Luke)

Happens to the best of us......the nurse will be in to feed her soon.

LUKE

O.K.....I'm about to leave....Can I just get a moment?

DOCTOR

By all means...please let me leave you two.

Doctor Adams walks offstage. Luke walks over to his seat, sits down and stares at Sarah's unconscious body. After a few moments he stands up and gets by her side. By this time heart rate and vital signs can be heard throughout the audience on the electrocardiograph monitor. Luke picks up a cord connected to the

> machine and holds it in his hand. He leans over and kisses Sarah on her forehead.

LUKE

Never have to say sorry huh? Doesn't sound too bad.

> Lights fade and the sound of the vital signs go flat

Play Ends

IV. Just another Day

> A ridiculously loud alarm clock could be heard constantly ringing while a half sleep, half comatose Isaac and Julia lay tangled together on a loveseat. Isaac gets up, begrudgingly to turn off the alarm clock. Somewhat gently, he lifts Julia's limp body off of him. Simultaneously the same alarm clock wakes up Clarissa and she gets up to feed her 6 month old son. The lights focus in on Isaac and Julia's half of the stage while Clarissa is on

the other half carrying out mommy duties. Isaac stumbles to the counter and looks back toward Julia before he begins ransacking her purse for prescription pills. He grabs what's left of a beer from the night before and chugs the rest of after throwing what looked like a handful of skittles in his mouth .Isaac hears Julia's phone ringing and throws it offstage while he makes his way back to the couch and lays down back down. Isaac's movements upon getting back onto the couch happen to wake Julia.

JULIA

(Really Groggy)

Ahhh....What time is it?

ISAAC

I dunno..think it's around 9

Stage lights then begin to focus in on Isaac and Julia while simultaneously Clarissa carries out her mommy duties and

>   takes her time preparing for
>   work.

                        JULIA

Nine...Shit! Shit! Shit! I'm supposed to open up and my parents are coming in today.

>   Julia hastily gets up trying to
>   find all of her belongings with
>   her eye on making her way to
>   the door.

                        ISAAC

I'm pretty sure they got somebody to cover you.

                        JULIA

I haven't been late Isaac, I can't. I can't be late today. Especially for nothing.

                        ISAAC

Just don't go in today//

                        JULIA

I can't Isaac. That's it. I just can't...I don't have any more sick days. We all can't live like this. I gotta go get dressed up at my place.

                        ISAAC

I gotta shower here//

                        JULIA

Uhhh no....Have you seen your restroom?......Look last night was...yeah I don't want you to think too much of what happened//

ISAAC

//This again? Really?...You come over here use me...which I'm ok with and leave. I get it.

JULIA

I'm just saying Isaac. I just want to be clear THIS (as she points to herself and Isaac) isn't something serious. We have fun and all but that's....that's about it.

ISAAC

What does it take to get you to take me seriously?

> Julia is still gathering her belongings. She doesn't look Isaac in the eye while talking; she just keeps avoiding eye contact.

JULIA

More

ISAAC

More what?//

JULIA

(As she points around the apartment)

More than this uhhh//

ISAAC

Stop just stop. You don't even know me.

JULIA

There's nothing to know. Living like this they're will never be nothing to know. I can't even tell my friends about this.

ISAAC

What do your friends matter? Is my life really that crappy?

> As he says this, a man in a large rat/mouse suit comes out and walks pass Isaac and Julia opens up the fridge and starts making a sandwich both Isaac and Julia look up at him slightly perturbed.

RICQUO

I'm sorry am I interrupting something?

ISAAC/JULIA

(Both in unison)

YES!

JULIA

(Under her breath to Isaac)

I thought you got rid of your mice problem?

ISAAC

I told you that last time. I couldn't afford it. I can't afford anything right now. It was either pay for that or not eat for a while so I decided I liked food more than I disliked rats.

RICQUO

Sorry....It's just that I ordered something from amazon and I haven't got it//

ISAAC

Ricquo....not now. Please...not now.

JULIA

(Under her breath to Isaac)

Ricquo? He has a name? These mice you have are pretty bold.......and abnormally large.

ISAAC

Oh Well he's a rat. And he's from New York.

> Both of them nod their head as if that's a good enough reason for Ricquo to be an abnormally large rat...and talking

JULIA

(As she watches Ricquo in total disgust)

This…..this is your roommate.

> Ricquo makes his way to the couch and turns on the TV to ESPN while stuffing his face with his sandwich. He props his feet on the table and lets out a loud belch.

JULIA

(With a look of total repulsion on her face)

……I gotta go.

ISAAC

Do you want your stuff back?

JULIA

What?

ISAAC

Your stuff

JULIA

What stuff?

ISAAC

Your leather whip...rope...handcuffs...and these anal beads//

                        RICQUO

Oh yeah sorry those are mine...Long weekend.

                        Ricquo gets up from the couch and grabs the anal beads from Isaac. He takes a whiff of them.

                        RICQUO

Mmmm...Sarah that scent never gets old.

                        Julia walks back and quickly grabs her stuff before heading out.

                        ISAAC

Can I get a name...a real name this time...or at least know where you work?

                        JULIA

Next time....

                        She makes her way to the door with Isaac following her. When Isaac goes in to kiss her she stops him short of kissing her.

                        JULIA

Isaac. That was yesterday...todays today.

> She walks away leaving Isaac and Isaac's face still in search for a kiss.

RICQUO

(Still eating a sandwich)

Fuck that bitch. She's not good for us bro.

ISAAC

She's using me.....

RICQUO

For sex? What's the problem?

> A loud knocking could be heard at the door again. Isaac's attention turns toward the door.

ISAAC

Ahh! Knew she would change her mind!

> Isaac opens the door only to find an notice to with red print. He looks at it intently before opening it up.

ISAAC

Eviction notice? The hell is this? Ricquo I thought you covered the last couple of months. You said you wrote a traveler's check.

RICQUO

You thought I was serious? Bro...I'm a rat. I don't have a checking account... I did have some money but I spent it all on cheese that night so I really don't remember much....saw one of my cousins get killed the night before so I went all out....Made me tear up that that type of violence didn't even make the damn news.

> Pushing the impending eviction to the back if his head in order to console Ricquo, Isaac heads toward the couch and sits next to him.

ISAAC

I'm sorry to hear. What happened to him?

RICQUO

(Sniffling)

Mouse trap to the neck....sick bastards.

> Ricquo starts to weep obnoxiously

He had 426 kids....all of 'em have to grow up without a father....such a cruel world.

> Suddenly a phone could be heard ringing. Isaac and Ricquo both begin looking around to see where the sound is coming from. After pulling out objects that should never be inside of a couch like a blender, toaster and canoe they find Julia's phone in between the couch of the apartment.

ISAAC

She left her phone! Maybe she did on purpose so she has to come back.

RICQUO

Or because she was trying to leave so fast she left it...but hey let's hope for the best.

ISAAC

Oh she'll be back//

RICQUO

Yeah with a restraining order.

ISAAC

They'll be nowhere for her to come back since we're getting kicked out anyways. Could I stay with you if I get kicked out?

RICQUO

Yeah definitely...I got somewhere we could go inside of the ceiling of this one place//

ISAAC

//Nevermind....we gotta figure something out.

> Ricquo lifts up the bong in an attempt to pass it to Isaac

ISAAC

Not right now bro...I gotta figure this out.

RICQUO

Don't let that shit get to you. This'll help ya day. Release ya chakras and shit. C'mon man.

> Isaac waits for a second then hesitantly grabs the bong. Isaac takes a rip starts coughing heavily and eases into the couch.

RICQUO

(While Isaac is coughing)

Yeah that's what I'm talkin about.

ISAAC

Damn...what is this? You said its blue dream?

RICQUO

Blue dream? No I meant blue cheese.

Isaac gets up quickly and slightly perturbed. In the process he happens to knock Riqcuo's bong over.

ISAAC

C'mon Bro//

RICQUO

//No no !

ISAAC

I'm sorry man I didn't mean to. You shoulda told me that was freakin' cheese dude. I thought it was weed.

RICQUO

You broke Billy Bong Thornton!

Ricquo goes over to the pieces and tries to put them back together. He starts talking to the bong while picking up the pieces. Ricquo is

>   letting tears out as if
>   he's standing over a
>   dead friend's body
>   trying to keep them
>   alive.

                        RICQUO

Billy I'm sorry…hold on man…breathe just breathe.

                        ISAAC

It's a bong bro…It's not alive.

                        RICQUO

Don't you talk to billy like that…billy didn't do nothing to you!

                        ISAAC

I'm sorry man. Jeez…It's glass though.

                        RIQCUO

MURDERER!

                        ISAAC

Look mann…I'll get you a new one.

                        RICQUO

New one? You can't just replace someone who's been there through the thick and thin. I don't want a new one. I want Billy!

>   Isaac feels horrible
>   about breaking the
>   bong and stumbles

over his words for a second trying to make Ricquo feel better.

                    ISAAC

If..If I could get you some cheese would that help?

Ricquo's sobbing begins to lighten up immediately when he hears this.

                    RICQUO

                    (Still sniffling)

Well...I guess that'll help ease the pain.

Wade walks in during this exchange on the phone. Throughout his phone conversation Wade goes to the fridge and sits on the couch still talking on the phone. Wade throws a bag of tacos to Isaac.

                    WADE

                    (Laughing)

This is for yall. Yeah it was crazy ass party. So like I'm balls deep in this midget chick. This is where shit gets wild. I'm just about to nut and her dog comes up from behind. Usually I would've stopped but I was about to climax so I kept going and the dog starts lickin my balls. This ten seconds like lasted forever because I'm just about to nut and the biggest ethical dilemma of our generation comes up. Do I finish while this dog is licking my balls?

> Isaac and Ricquo look at each other.

ISAAC

(To wade)

That's actually considered beastiality in some states.

RICQUO

Oh you too good to have a dog lick ya balls but you ain't too good to charge a rat for rent?

> Wade covers the phone and whispers to Isaac and Ricquo.

WADE

(With hand over the phone)

He does have a point.

ISAAC

Fuck both of ya'll.

> Wade lets out a light chuckle then returns to his phone conversation.

                                WADE

                           (On the phone)

Look I gotta go. Imma stop by later and pick up those pills. I need those....What? You told me I could have a few for free since you jipped me on the weed I bought from you. Ok that works. Love you too grandma. Tell Deacon Williams I said hi.

                                              Wade hangs up his
                                              phone puts his feet up
                                              on the table.

                                WADE

Fuck's up guys?

                                ISAAC

Whats up man?

                                              Wade grabs an apple
                                              and bites into it.

                                WADE

My cholesterol...but besides that everything. It's a good day. You know why it's a good day?

                                ISAAC

Because you haven't had a heart attack yet...

                                WADE

Well that too...but because we're gonna make money...the moolah...the big bucks...pesos...you know the good stuff!

ISAAC

Another get rich quick scheme? Like the bacon floss? Or the edible onesies?

> Scene changes to a confessional room like that that's been scene on real world or the office.

ISAAC

It's kinda hard taking Wade seriously, because when ya do you forget who Wade is. I mean….I love the guy but sometimes he might put you in a bad predicament.

> Scene changes to Isaac in the woods walking around with a suit on and a briefcase. He is on the phone with Wade.

ISAAC

You sure this is where I'm supposed to meet up? It's just that I've never had an interview in the middle of the woods.

WADE

(On the other end of the phone)

Yeah trust me. Found em on craigslist. My cousin says their up and coming with a lot of growing room in their company. I've heard they're one of those pyramid style companies. Get to network and meet some new people.

> Isaac is on the phone with his briefcase in one hand phone in the other walking through the woods slowly. He pulls out a business card.

ISAAC

It's just...I don't know. Sheisty traveling services...that doesn't sound a little off to you? And the place he picked for an interview? I mean I'm in the woods.

WADE

Maybe they're like one of those creative companies that just want to see if you're really interested.

> Isaac sees a man with a trench coat and sunglasses. This guy is attempting to look inconspicuous, but how inconspicuous can you really look in the woods with a trench coat and glasses on...at night. Scene goes back to confession room.

ISAAC

If ya can't tell I wasn't too keen on accepting their job offer. Let's not mention the science experiment his cousin used my apartment for when I asked him to house sit my dog.

Scene goes to apartment with mountains of chemicals on table with Wade in a toxic hazmat suit like the one used in Breaking Bad.

Wade is tinkering with the chemicals.

                  WADE

Man...Walter White makes this look a lot easier.

Isaac opens the door of his apartment with traveling bags. He puts his bags on the floor and starts looking around. Another guy is a toxic hazmat suit walks out of the restroom with a large pot with boiling steaming liquid in it.

                  ISAAC

The hell is going on?

                  WADE

Uhhh...research?

> Other guy in Hazmat suit speaks very fast Spanish while slowly putting the boiling water down little by little and walks away then when he is almost out of sight he could be seen running away.

ISAAC

Who the fuck is that? And what the fuck is going on?

> Scene goes back to Isaac's apt

WADE

Well I was going to wait till I was finished to tell you. I thought you'd be supportive that I was starting my own business. That's what friends do. Support each other.

ISAAC

Friends don't cook meth in other friend's kitchens.

WADE

Geez...Negative Nancy over here. You're so pessimistic about everything. Give optimism a try for a bit. We might not get fucked over like we did on our last business venture.

ISAAC

Wait...what business venture?

WADE

Remember when I found out the best way to make money was to actually make money. It was a great plan until you screwed me over and your printer ran out ink//

ISAAC

You were making counterfeit money from my house?

WADE

Yeah...isn't that genius? If you actually get some more ink I can get that going again.

ISAAC

I'm feeling sick right now.

WADE

Sometimes dog meat does that to me too. Taste so good though.

ISAAC

The hell are you talking about?

WADE

The tacos...they're dog meat.

ISAAC

You gave me fuckin dog meat too? What the fuck Wade?!

>   Isaac gets up and runs
>   to the restroom. He
>   slams the door and
>   could be heard
>   vomiting through the
>   door. Wade gets up
>   and tries to talk to him
>   while he is throwing
>   up.

                        WADE

Hey its gluten free! You're gonna be fine!

>   Louder vomiting noises
>   can be heard through
>   the door.

                        WADE

Look let's not dwell on the past...I've had a few hiccups but this is something different. THIS is a get rich in 24 hours plan. You won't have to do anything...I promise. It could help get the girl you've been talking about too.

>   Isaac opens the door
>   and looks at Wade

                        ISAAC

I'm listening....

WADE

My neighbor...I took her keys.

ISAAC

What about your neighbor?

WADE

The one that works at the bank I think I told you about. I took her keys.

ISAAC

I'm still not following you.

WADE

Dude...my neighbor. The one that works at the bank. I saw her leaving the complex and she dropped her keys and didn't even notice. I made copies of all of them. She has the keys to the safe. All we have to do is//

ISAAC

Whoa..now ya lost me. I'm not going down that road again. I got less than 6 more months till I'm off probation for our last adventure.

WADE

Hey ok who woulda known you couldn't travel on an airplane with fireworks? I'm saying it was the fourth of July and Its un-American to not have fireworks. You would think AMERICAN AIRLINES would understand that. Just try to trust me for a sec. This would literally be like stealing candy from a baby.

RICQUO

You'd be surprised that's a lot harder than you//

ISAAC

Ricquo...not now.

WADE

Hear me out for a bit...lookin at how ya apartment looks you can obviously use the money.

ISAAC

No...I'm done. No more...Nada I'm good.

WADE

What if I told you that you didn't have to do anything? (beat) I'll do everything. You keep all your cheddar.

ISAAC

I'd still have to do something//

> Ricquo begins shredding cheese in a grater and putting it in lines. He takes a straw and sniffs a large line of cheese.

RICQUO

Whoo! Damn that's good mozzarella! Cheddar? I like cheddar? What exactly would I have to do?

>Ricquo tries to pass the plate with lines of cheese around but Isaac and Wade both refuse his offer.

>   WADE

I'm good man. I only smoke weed

>A loud bullshit from Isaac could be heard on his way back to the restroom.

>   WADE

And cocaine every once in a while when I'm drunk. Don't really like it though...just the way it smells.

>   RICQUO

I tried cocaine before….for about 9 years. Didn't do it for me. This shit right here though. Its aged man…finest blue cheese out there. You gotta try it.

>   WADE

Naw man I'm good.

>   ISAAC

I'm cool too. Preciate ya though.

RICQUO

Fine...more for me.

> Ricquo sniffs up the remaining lines and begins to make obnoxious noises after each one while Isaac and Wade continue their conversation.

WADE

Look trust me. This plan is full proof. I've been watching her for some weeks now and I know her schedule. I know what time the bank closes and when they do their deposits for the day. She doesn't even work today so it'll be even better.

ISAAC

I don't know man...seems kinda off wouldn't ya say? Even for you mann....you don't think its wrong? No one on the inside ya know?

> As he is talking Ricquo's sounds keep getting obnoxiously louder to the point where they can't ignore him anymore

ISAAC

Aye man. Maybe you should slow down on the cheese//

> Ricquo's eyes are bugged out while he is talking to them now. He has a slight twitch as well.

RIQCUO

Look man it's not that bad for you. Plus I don't have a problem with cheese. I have a solution!

> Ricquo puts some cheese in a spoon and begins to light it while addressing Wade.

Now about that bank....What do we have to do?

WADE

(As he shrugs away Riqcuo's problem)

All we gotta do is go in when the bank's closed. I've been scoping 'em out for a while now. Not to say that I've been thinking about this for a while but when you walk by it every day you start to see how it works ya know?

ISAAC

Just sounds too good to be true.

WADE

So does winning the lottery but people do it all the time//

ISAAC

So we're comparing this to winning the lottery?? Oh yeah the odds are definitely in our favor now.

RIQCUO

(As he lights up a spoon)

Blue fuckin cheese

Both watch Ricquo as he straps a belt around his arm.

RICQUO

What? What?! It's just cheese bro...chill out.

WADE

Bro...you don't think you're going a bit overboard?

RICQUO

It's not a drug bro...don't be so square.

Ricquo grabs a syringe and puts some blue cheese from the spoon in it. Flicks the syringe a couple times and injects it in his arm.

RICQUO

(His eyes roll to the back of his head for a bit)

Ahh now that's the good shit...Now the bank.

> Isaac and Wade are still in looking at Ricquo in awe because he literally just injected cheese into his arm. Scene changes to Clarissa's phone ringing. Clarissa walks to her phone and answers it.

CLARISSA

Hello?......Hey Jerry. Yeah I'm still in town. Oh nothing much. Just feeding Alex about to drop him off at his grandmother's. Today? I'm off. Where's Julia? (Beat) Did you keep calling her?.....O.K I'm supposed to be off so I can't tell you I'm going to rush there. Give me an hour or so to get dressed and I can be there after I get some groceries.

> Clarissa gets her things together and double checks the apartment as she attempts to leave hastily. Scene goes back to Isaac's apt. Wade,k Ricquo and Isaac are sitting around smoking weed. They're all obviously high. Isaac's phone rings and

                                he looks ta but outs it
                                back down when he
                                looks at the call screen.

                    WADE

Ignoring people nowadays...who is it?

                    ISAAC

Fuckin probation officer....probably to make my last payment.

                                His phone vibrates
                                again indicating that he
                                has received a
                                voicemail.

                    ISAAC

One more month and I'm a free man. Feels good to just stay out of trouble and now I'm finally at the finish line.

                    WADE

Let's just hope it ain't for a drug test.

                    ISAAC

Man I ain't worried bout no damn drug test. She said as long as I stay current with my payments I won't have to worry about it.

                                While doing this wade
                                is pulling out his phone
                                getting ready to play
                                his voicemail. That's
                                when his phone rings
                                and he listens to his

                              voicemail of his
                              probation officer telling
                              him his next scheduled
                              drug test.

                    ISAAC

I got to take a drug test.

                              Wade takes a hit of the
                              joint.

                    WADE

I'll piss for ya.

                    ISAAC

I'm good on that man. Preciate ya though.

                    WADE

Anytime. That's what friends do.

                              Wade reaches his fist
                              out trying to get a fist
                              bump but Isaac leaves
                              him hanging.

                    ISAAC

Man what should I do?

                    RICQUO

I think you should start off with maybe stop smoking

ISAAC

Oh yeah ricquo?...I should stop? The day before?! You're the one who told me not to worry about it. You told me you've been in and out of the system in New York.

RICQUO

That's your fault. I never said I was arrested or anything. You took me out of context. I said "growing up in the streets of New York taught me a lot". I'm a fuckin rat. I literally grew up in the streets of New York.

ISAAC

Ah shit shit shit......Hold on for a second.

WADE

Just give her extra money. I'm pretty sure she'd be willing to work something out.

WADE

When you got money...the world is open and heaven is at your feet.

RICQUO

Ya know...I like the way you think. That's the same thing my dad told me...well before he got caught in that mouse trap in the liquor cabinet. But that's beside the story...Let's make it happen. We gotta pay rent right? And I can just picture all the cheese I can buy after we're done.

> Isaac gets on his phone and calls her again. He goes to the backroom.

                              Ricquo and Wade are
                              sitting on the couch
                              sharing a bag of hot
                              fries. Ricquo jumps up
                              as if he has the best
                              idea in the world.

                                    RICQUO

I got it! I think I can get into the back without anyone seeing me. Just send me in there to scope it out before it closes. With my ninja like reflexes they wouldn't even know I'm there.

                                    WADE

You think so?

                                    RICQUO

Mothafucka I know so. They used to call me real quiet Ricquo.

                                    WADE

Really now?

                                    RICQUO

Look this pussy ain't gonna do it. Let's get in and out. Get the money get some bitches and some cheese afterwards. You ever get a bitch to lick cheese of you?

                                    WADE

Nah….not at all

                                    RICQUO

Aww mann....you ain't livin.

                    RICQUO

Bitches love parmesan! That's beside the point though. You wanna do this or nah? Let your juevos hang for a bit and let's take what the world has out there for us.

                    WADE

Do you actually have balls?

                    RICQUO

It's a metaphor dick!

                    WADE

Oh...Im sorry. I'm with ya.

                    RICQUO

I like that answer. 50/50 split. Now let's help this guy out. Take Isaac to get some cranberry juice to try and clean his system. Here I'll give you some money.

> Ricquo walks to his wallet and pulls out some monopoly money.

I think this should be enough. Ya'll get something to eat while y'all are out. Get me some string cheese while y'all are out. Need to have some for going out tonight.

> Wade looks down at the money is about to

> tell Ricquo this money isn't worth anything but just puts it in his pocket and goes to grab Isaac.

> RICQUO

And a slushie too! It's happy hour.

> Scene goes to Isaac and Wade walking through the grocery store.

> WADE

We're gonna be Oprah rich!

> ISAAC

It just seems a little off still…I dunno man seems too good to be true. Isaac seems disinterested in Wade's emphatic convo. Isaac walks down the water aisle aisle and begins putting gallons of water and cranberry juice in his grocery cart. He then walks toward the juice aisle to get some cranberry juice.

> ISAAC

Can't believe it came down to this bullshit.

> WADE

What? This isn't my last option like we've done before. This one is my first. I'm telling you I've been watching the flow of everything for a while now//

> At this moment Clarissa turns down the aisle as well. Isaac is front of her with his back to him yelling at Wade.

ISAAC

I'm not talking about your fucking stupid little plan Wade. I'm talking about the bullshit I'm going through now because of you. All because you packed too many clothes and decided to put YOUR fireworks in my luggage without telling me. I swear to god if I get my shit revoked cause of you I'm gonna fuckin strangle you.

> Clarissa notices Isaac and does her best to not get seen by Isaac or Wade while getting her stuff.

WADE

Look bro....I'm sorry. If I could trade places with you I would. I promise.

ISAAC

Me too.

WADE

Why don't you just get some fake pee?

ISAAC

Ya know? That's probably the best idea you've had all day.

                    ISAAC

Where would we get some at?

                    WADE

From someone you know or smoke shops. I would go with the smoke shop though. They're a bit more reliable//

                    ISAAC

Where is one at? The closest one I mean.

                    WADE

Let's figure it out.

                                        Both pull out their
                                        smartphones and begin
                                        googling locations.

                    ISAAC

One is literally a few miles from here.

                    WADE

We got a winner.

                    ISAAC

Fuck. We gotta go back and get Ricquo. I promised I would buy him a new bong. I fuckin broke his earlier today.

                    WADE

Whatever we do, let's get to it.

> Isaac and Wade jog out of the store. Clarissa could be seen behind them hiding like where's waldo. Scene goes back to Isaac's apt. Ricquo is by himself. He is just getting out the shower with a shower cap on.

RICQUO

(Singing to himself)

MMM...bitches love ricquo. They be like Riqcuo come have my baby.

> Ricquo looks at himself in the mirror.

RICQUO

(To himself)

Damn I look good! ain't another rat alive that got it going on like this.

> Does a few dances in the mirror. Suddenly a loud knock can be heard.

RICQUO

Who the fuck is that? Knocking like the police and shit.

> Ricquo makes his way to the door still with his shower cap on.

                    RICQUO

              (While walking to the door)

Got damn no respect....The hell.

> Ricquo opens the door. Julia is standing there.

                    JULIA

Sorry to intrude or disturb. I just seem to have left my phone and I was hoping it was still here//

                    RICQUO

//Yeah yeah come in...I saw it somewhere.

> Knock at the door can be heard again.

                    RICQUO

The hell?...

> Ricquo walks to the door and opens it. It's a man reading from a note card with a baseball card and sunglasses on.

                    CREEPER

Hello. My name is John Ashton. I am here to inform you that I am a registered sex offender//

JULIA

John? Is that you?

JOHN/CREEPER

Julia is that you? Oh my god it's been forever.

> John lets himself in the apartment and walks right past ricquo bumping him slightly while making his way to hug Julia.

JULIA

How have you been?//

RICQUO

//First off who the hell are you? And can you please get the hell outta my house?

JOHN/CREEPER

I'm so sorry. I'm your new neighbor. Just moved in and doing my rounds in the building. What's your name?

RICQUO

I'm Ricquo.

>   John holds out his hand
>   and when Ricquo
>   extends his for a
>   handshake, john pulls
>   him closer and kisses
>   his hand.

JOHN/CREEPER

(While giving Ricquo a creepy look)

The pleasure is all mine....You know I've heard once you go rat you never go back. Is it true?

RICQUO

I think you should probably get going now. I'm pretty sure a task force is looking for you out there somewhere.

>   Julia walks John to the
>   door.

JULIA

Not to sound rushed but I'm sorry I got to go to work. I had no idea you stayed here john. We need to catch up sometime.

JOHN/CREEPER

Yes we do. We should have some coffee....And you...any time you need some sugar I'll be right over here...2346. See you soon neighbor.

>   Julia closes the door
>   behind the new

>   neighbor. She saunters
>   back over by Ricquo.

            JULIA

Sorry about that.

            RICQUO

How do ya'll know each other?

>   Julia starts with the
>   side eyes

            JULIA

Uhhh...we both partake in similar activities. Ya know...Yoga...sculpting and he's in my book club. That sort of thing.

            RICQUO

That motherfucka was weird.

            JULIA

Yeah he's a little...different.

>   Ricquo completely over
>   the situation walks
>   back to the table and
>   begins slicing up some
>   cheese.

            RICQUO

You want some?

            JULIA

No I'm fine. I'm not hungry.

>	Ricquo continues to break down the cheese.

>	RICQUO

Yeah me neither...

>	Ricquo forms a large line of cheese and put his nose to it.

>	RICQUO

Whooo! That's what daddy needs. You sure you don't need any?

>	The whole time Julia has been looking curiously at Ricquo.

>	JULIA

You make it seem so fun.

>	RICQUO

This shit right here. Ah mann...It's like a cross between an orgasm and turning super saiyan. Best feeling in the world.

>	Ricquo pours out some more broken down cheese and just throws his face into i.

>	RICQUO

Ahh now this is heaven.

>Julia walks over to the couch and sits next to Ricquo.

RICQUO

Your turn. You're gonna love it.

>Julia puts her face to the place sniffs it and before putting it up her nose she realizes it's really cheese

JULIA

This is really cheese.

RICQUO

Of course it is bitch. What did you think it was?

JULIA

Nothing.

>She grabs a little bit and chews it.

JULIA

This is really good cheese though I must say.

RICQUO

It goes better with some wine.

                                    Scene goes silent with
                                    shots of dialogue
                                    between ricquo and
                                    Julia obviously turning
                                    friendly while ricquo
                                    binges on some more
                                    cheese.

                    JULIA

              (Swirling her wine glass)

So I have to ask. Is it true?

                    RICQUO

I told you...It was me and Robert Downey Jr who threw the party.

                    JULIA

No not that...

                    RICQUO

What else?

                    JULIA

You know...Is it true? Once you go rat you never go back.

                    RICQUO

Only one way to find out wouldn't ya say?

                                    Ricquo pulls out
                                    a bottle of

parmesan cheese

RICQUO

Come take it off me.

Julia lets out a smile and grabs the puppet they make their way behind the couch and scene fades to black.

Scene 3

Isaac and Wade are at the front of the apartment waiting on Ricquo. They are locked out of the apartment complex.

ISAAC

The hell is taking him so damn long.

WADE

Is he here?

ISAAC

He should be. Knock again.

Some noises can be heard inside. A girls

>   laughter could be heard
>   getting closer to the
>   door.

>   ISAAC

The fuck?

>   Isaac puts his ear closer
>   to the door. While he is
>   pressed up against it
>   Julia walks out bumping
>   directly into him.

>   ISAAC

Julia?

>   JULIA
>
>   (Awkwardly)

Oh hey. I left my phone earlier...I had to pick it up. Ricquo let me in and helped me find it.

>   ISAAC

Oh. That's cool. I'm actually really glad to see you again. Wanna go get some drinks later tonight?

>   JULIA

Uhh...I don't know. I'll call you later though.

>   Julia walks out of the
>   doorway as quickly as
>   possible.

ISAAC

Ok bye. Talk to you later.

> Isaac goes in for a hug but by the time he puts his arms out he can grasp nothing but air as she already left.

WADE

She must be really late for work.

> Wade walks into the apartment followed by Isaac. Ricquo walks out of the room unaware that Isaac and Wade have come back.

RICQUO

Baby! That thing with your tong...oh hey guys.

WADE

What you been up to man? Where you been? We have been calling you since we left the store.

RICQUO

Oh...I went to my yoga classes.

> Wade and Isaac in unison

Yoga?

RICQUO

What a rat can't release his chakras and get all flexible without being judged?

            WADE

No it's not that...I just never mind

            RICQUO

Never mind what? Might as well say it now.

            ISAAC

It's nothing bro...Look we found out where to get some stuff that'll help me tomorrow. It's at the smoke shop. We can pick you up a new bong to.

            RICQUO

I guess I'll ride. I'm calling shotgun though. Trying to stretch out. Let me finish getting dressed though.

            ISAAC

Why does it smell like baby oil?

            RICQUO

Oh that...It's good for ya skin. Yeah that's it.

>   Ricquo walks back to the room leaving Isaac and Wade in the living room waiting on him to get dressed. Thinking its going to take forever Wade starts to make a

                              sandwich. Ricquo
                              pretty quickly walks out
                              with nothing changed
                              about his appearance
                              while Wade is still
                              making the sandwich.

                    RICQUO

Ok. Let's go.

                    WADE

Motherfucker

Scene 4

                              Isaac, Wade, and
                              Ricquo enter the smoke
                              shop. Isaac and Wade
                              begin to walk around
                              the smoke shop looking
                              at pipes through the
                              glass. Ricquo sticks his
                              face up to the glass of
                              one of the displays.

                    RICQUO

This one looks like you could fit about a quarter of some blue cheese in this one. Ah shit.

                              Store teller walks in
                              from the back.

                          ATTENDANT

How ya doing gentlemen?

                                    Wade walks over to the
                                    sales attendant

                          WADE

Hey do you guys sell fake pee? You know the types to pass a drug test.

                          ATTENDANT

Sir we don't deal with aiding false reports for a drug test. We do however sell synthetic urine for any purpose.

                          ISAAC

Ok. What's your best synthetic urine you guys carry?

                                    The sales attendant
                                    walks over and shows
                                    Isaac some different
                                    options.

                          ATTENDANT

This one right here sir happens to be the most commonly used one by our customers.

                          ISAAC

Ok. Let me get one of those and the other one right there.

                                    Isaac points at one
                                    beyond the counter.

ATTENDANT

Would that be all for you sir?

ISAAC

No my friend is looking to by a bong he might need some help with his selection.

> Sales attendant walks over to Ricquo

ATTENDANT

Is there anything I can help you with sir?

RICQUO

Yeah which one of these burns cheese the best?

ATTENDANT

I'm sorry sir I didn't catch that.

RICQUO

Cheese…Ya know what you put on a pizza.

ATTENDANT

UHHH//

RICQUO

Motherfuckin cheese…that good shit. Nevermind. Let me get that one right there.

> Ricquo points to a bong. The attendant gets it through the

> glass and brings it to the counter with the rest of Isaac's stuff that he's buying. The attendant begins to ring it all up.

ATTENDANT

The total for that would be 257 dollars and 49 cents.

RICQUO

You guys take travelers checks?

> Sales person looks at him curiously

ATTENDANT

I'm sorry sir unfortunately we don't.

RICQUO

Its fine. I have cash.

> Ricquo pulls out a wad of monopoly money.

You said 257 right?

> Ricquo begins fumbling through the cash.

Hate dealing with cash

ATTENDANT

Uhhh....

> Ricquo tries to hand the cashier 3 monopoly 100's.

RICQUO

Here ya go. Keep the change.

ATTENDANT

I'm sorry sir we don't accept Monopoly money either.

RICQUO

The hell? Y'all don't except travelers checks or paper money? What kind of establishment is this?

> Ricquo begins to raise his voice and yell at the attendant.

RICQUO

My money ain't good here is what you tryin to tell me? This is America!

> Isaac comes between Ricquo and the sales attendant.

ISAAC

I'm sorry sir. My friend here has been having a bad day.

ATTENDANT

I don't know what y'all think or if this is some type of joke but//

RICQUO

//Bad day? I'll show you a bad day! What time you get off man?

ATTENDANT

I'm going to ask your friend to leave for the last time.

RICQUO

RIQCUO DON'T PLAY THAT SHIT!

ATTENDANT

Ok. You two and the rat. Out now.

> Ricquo is still yelling irately when the attendant makes his way to the phone. He picks it up and starts dialing.

ATTENDANT

Hello yes I like to request for an officer at our location. We have some customers that won't leave.

> Slight hold in conversation.

Yes mam. Two males and a rat. I think the rat is also in possession of some narcotics. He keeps talking about this cheese substance.

ISAAC

Ricquo let's go!

> All three of them run out of the shop while

the attendant is still on the phone.

Scene 5

All three walk back into the apartment arguing about what previously happened.

          ISAAC

You didn't have to charge the guy up man.

          RICQUO

He just didn't like me. He coulda took my money. I've never had a problem before.

          ISAAC

What the hell did you give him?

          RICQUO

300...

          ISAAC

300 dollars? So what was the issue? By the time I got that you guys were already yelling at the top of your lungs.

          RICQUO

It's cause I'm a rat.

          WADE

Nah I think it's because you gave him monopoly money//

                            ISAAC

You gave him monopoly money?

                            RICQUO

I gave him the money I've been saving for some years now. My parents left me little bit before they left.

                            WADE

So your parents left you monopoly money?

                            RICQUO

Look I don't know what monopoly is. My parents were pretty well off. When my father died the will left me everything in his cupboard.

                            ISAAC

This motherfucker is trippin....Ricquo let me see your cash.

>   Still unhappily grumbling about the experience at the smoke shop Ricquo walks over and gets his wallet and gives it to Isaac. Isaac grabs it and pulls out 100 dollar monopoly bills. Isaac lets out a deep sigh.

                            ISAAC

Fuckin idiot...so this is what you paid rent withb the last couple months?

RICQUO

Yeah...I aint ever had a problem with it before.

ISAAC

Oh god.

Isaac begins pacing back and forth

RICQUO

Well come to think of I never really paid rent before.

ISAAC

Ricquo...this isn't real money.

RICQUO

The hell you talkin about?

ISAAC

This!

He holds up the money in his hand

Isn't real money. It's used for board games.

RICQUO

The hell its not. You just used it to buy all that damn cranberry juice and water earlier today//

WADE

Yeah sorry about that...I shoulda told you when you handed it to me. I just didn't want to hurt your feelings.

ISAAC

Got damn...now it all makes sense.

RICQUO

So wait...you trying to tell me...I'm broke.

ISAAC

If this is all you have then hell fuckin yes your broke as shit.

> Isaac grabs the money balls it up and throws it on the floor.

God damn.

RICQUO

Well at least we're getting some real money tonight right?

ISAAC

We? I'm not doing shit with this idiot.

> He points at Wade. Wade was trying to catch a mosquito in the air during the conversation

WADE

Huh?

ISAAC

Ya'll can have a blast with that.

Isaac walks out of the room.

RICQUO

Alright...fuck you too then.

Wade and Isaac make their way to the couch and sit down. They begin smoking a joint.

RICQUO

Let's get it. That real shit. Ya know?

WADE

Let's do it. We're like Butch Cassidy and the Sundance Kid...or like like Bonnie and Clyde.

RICQUO

Or like billy the kid

WADE

You think we need a name for us? How bout the two amigos?

RICQUO

How about pretty Ricquo and his subpar sidekick. Kinda catchy you think?

> WADE

Eh...I'm not a big fan of that one. Maybe Ash/Pikachu? Since we're gonna catch em all.

>> Wade puts his fist in the air searching for a fist bump. Ricquo leaves him hanging.

> RICQUO

Who the fuck is Pikachu? I don't live in a fuckin ball asshole. How about Ricquo and the Ricquettes? That's kinda catchy. Yeah I like that one.

> WADE

It's only cool if we get away remember that.

>> Ricquo grabs the joint from Wade's hand.

> RICQUO

I know motherfucka. This shit is cake to a ninja assassin like myself. I got this.

>> Wade and Ricquo continue to smoke while thinking of names. The scene changes to Isaac

walking outside smoking a cigarette on the phone. He gets Julia's voicemail.

                    ISAAC

Hey just calling to see if you wanna hang out tonight. Call me back when you can. Bye.

Isaac puts his phone in his back pocket and sits on the curb and continues to smoke his cigarette. Suddenly his phone rings. He is surprised by it, looks at the screen lets out a big grin, gets a hold of his phone and inhales the cigarettes one last time and throws it down before picking it up.

                    ISAAC

Hey! I was wondering when you were gonna call me.

Isaac continues to walk on the sidewalk while on the phone.

No that's fine with me. Yeah when you get off just come over. Ricquo and Wade are leaving so we can have the place all to ourselves. Sounds great. See you soon.

> Isaac jumps up and down letting out a victory celebration. He is unaware that other people on the sidewalk are looking at him strangely.

ISAAC

(To the bystanders)

She loves me! Haha I knew it!

> He walks away smiling from ear to ear as happy as can be.

Scene 6

> Julia and Clarissa are behind their desks finishing up a withdrawal for a customer.

>Julia gets up to let out the last customer before locking the doors.

                    JULIA

Have a nice day!

>Julia locks the door behind the customer and walks back over her desk where Clarissa is counting the money. Julia starts helping her with the daily rituals of closing up the bank. While still counting the deposits for the day Clarissa begins to talk to Julia.

                    CLARISSA

You never told me what happened this morning.

                    JULIA

Sorry...There was this dog in this burning building so I stopped//

                    CLARISSA

Shut the fuck up.

JULIA

Well do you honestly really want to know or you just asking for the sake of asking?

CLARISSA

I wanna know.

JULIA

I kinda woke up late at my friend's house.

CLARISSA

Kinda?! You showed up an hour before we closed up. It 6 pm. You were supposed to be here at 9.

JULIA

Geez.... I didn't say I was right at all just telling you what happened.

CLARISSA

Sorry it's just that you shoulda//

JULIA

Hey captain hindsight...let not go there. What happened happened. I'm here.

CLARISSA

(Sarcastically)

Yeah let's not try to fix it. I sooooooo enjoy coming in on my off days I was just waiting by the phone holding my breath.

JULIA

See if I woulda showed up to work you woulda suffocated so gotta look at the bright side of everything.

> Clarissa glares at Julia in hopes to make a wittier comeback but doesn't quite come up with the retort she wants.

CLARISSA

C-CUNT!

JULIA

Whoa...where did that come from? What got up your skirt?

CLARISSA

Its...sorry I didn't mean it to come out like that. Life's been a little I guess what would be a synonym for hectic and chaotic?

JULIA

Fucked the fuck up

CLARISSA

I guess we'll go with that....Life's been a little fucked the fuck up the past week or so and I really just been trying to take it all in. Sarah's father got in contact with me...I don't know how//

MALCOLM

Who's there?!

> Malcolm a morbidly obese blind security guard puppet

>bursts into the bank and starts waving his walking stick through the air.

>CLARISSA

Malcolm! It's me and Julia we're just closing up. Just us. We'll be out in a few. I'll talk to you about it later

>MALCOLM

You ladies alright?

>CLARISSA

Yeah we're ok

>MALCOLM

No need to be in fear...Malcolm's here.

>Malcolm begins walking around the bank touching everything he can get in contact with trying to secure a bank as much as a blind man can. Julia and Clarissa both stare at each other for a short second

>JULIA

She said we're ok.

MALCOLM

What?!

JULIA

She said we're ok

MALCOLM

What?!

JULIA

SHE SAID WE'RE OK.

MALCOLM

What?!

CLARISSA

(Whispering to Julia)

He's a little hard of hearing as well.

JULIA

Aaaannnd this is our top flight security system?

CLARISSA

We hired him because we thought he was a veteran….When he told us he served for a bit in Japan we didn't think he was talking about a hotdog eating contest he was a waiter at. By the time we found out about it he was employed and loving his job and we kinda felt bad for him so…yeah that's our top flight security.

                        Both Clarissa and Julia
                        watch as Malcolm is
                        walking around the
                        bank bumping into an
                        obscene amount of
                        stuff on the stage.
                        Malcolm begins to
                        breathe heavily and
                        takes a seat by the
                        door and pulls out his
                        inhaler.

                              JULIA

Did ya'll really give this guy a gun too?

                        CLARISSA

At first...then he fired a couple rounds in the break room when someone opening the fridge behind him. He has really good sense of smell to make up for his lack of others one might say.

                        MALCOLM

Your deodorant smells lovely might I say Clarissa. I can see you had spinach tody as wel.. Way to eat healthy.

                        CLARISSA

Yeah spinach artichoke...Thanks Malcolm

                        JULIA

He can smell like that? Can he smell me as well?

                        CLARISSA

Mmmm...Probably. Let's find out. Hey Malcolm

                    MALCOLM

What?!

                    CLARISSA

Can you tell what Julia had for breakfast and lunch?

                    MALCOLM

Yeah a plate of shame and regret....and a large amount of cheese mixed with baby oil. I can't tell if you ate it or lathered it on you//

                    JULIA

OK! I get the point.

> Wade looks at Ricquo and he looks back at him with a big smile.

                    JULIA

So....he doesn't have a weapon. What does he actually do when someone attempts to//

                    CLARISSA

He has a whistle.

                    JULIA

                (Sarcastically)

Thank baby Jesus for the whistle! We'll all be saved.

CLARISSA

Why so negative? No one actually attempts to rob banks anymore anyways….that's back in the old days.

> Simultaneously while her and Julia are engaged in conversation Ricquo and Wade tiptoe like Elmer Fudd trying to catch roger rabbit past a sleeping Malcolm at the front door and hide behind a banker's desk.

With new technology and our top flight security over here we'll be ok. Plus no one is able to tell he's blind anyways.

> As she says this Ricquo is waving his hands over Malcolm's eyes. Wade pulls Ricquo just as Julia and Clarissa turn around to close up and walk out the bank.

JULIA

I don't know…I feel like we're setting ourselves up.

CLARISSA

We'll be ok…plus what's the worst that can happen? We're leaving Malcom. See ya tomorrow.

> Unaware that Clarissa is talking to him Malcolm is still sleep in a chair by the door.

JULIA

(Yelling)

MALCOLM….!

> Malcolm startled wakes up abruptly.

MALCOLM

Who's there?! I'm armed and dangerous!

JULIA

Freakin idiot…MALCOLM WE ARE LEAVING. WE. WILL. SEE. YOU. TOMORROW.

> While she is saying this Julia is making hand gestures that would appear as sign language but probably far from it.

MALCOLM

Ok..bye.

JULIA

Bye

MALCOLM

What?!

JULIA

I said bye

MALCOLM

What?!

JULIA

I said bye

MALCOLM

What?!

JULIA

I'm leaving.

Julia walks out the bank. Clarissa gives Malcolm a pat on the shoulder before they both exit the stage. At this moment Ricqcuo's ears can be seen rising up behind the desk. Him and Wade slowly

>rise up and begin tiptoeing slowly to the safe. Malcolm abruptly wakes up which freezes Malcolm and Ricquo in their place.

                    MALCOLM

I smell cheap cologne.

                    WADE

                (Whispering to Ricquo)

He can smell me?!

                    RICQUO

                (Whispering)

Cologne that crappy I'm surprised everybody can't.

>Malcolm makes his rounds around the bank searching for where the smell is coming from. Ricquo and Wade keep avoid bumping into him while Malcolm waddles his way around the bank. Malcolm pauses and takes another sniff.

                    MALCOLM

Is that gasoline?

>Ricquo looks at Wade.

WADE

(Whispering)

What? It's Black Panther cologne.

RICQUO

(Whispering to Wade)

Your horrible cologne is going to get us caught man.

WADE

(Whispering)

Don't fucking blame me. It's not my fault his spidey-senses are kicking in.

RICQUO

(Whispering)

Don't bring a man to do a rat's job. Look, just meet me at the car and give me the keys to the safe. Give me 5 minutes.

After a brief tug of war with the keys Wade gives the keys to Ricquo and tries to make his way out. All throughout the process Malcolm follows the scent of Wade to the door.

MALCOLM

Hmmm...Must have been the slut of a teller's stench.

> Riqcuo slowly sinks behind one of the desks and rises back up with a ninja mask.

RICQUO

The time has come.

> Riqcuo agilely moves toward the safe. Well as agilely as a large man in a rat suit can appear. Malcolm falls back asleep in his chair and can be heard snoring. Ricquo gets to the safe and puts his ear to it. After two tries he finally gets the safe open. The unlocking of the safe can be heard for a moment and Ricquo pauses. It is not enough to wake up a sleeping Malcolm.

RICQUO

(Whispering to himself while rubbing his hands together)

Now this...this is what I need.

> Ricquo begins to pull the cash out and stuff it into a bag and once it's full he begins to stuff it anywhere he can on his body. He kinda resembles the

guy who drives the boat and motorcycle that is made out of money on the Geico commercial right now the way it is falling out of his bag and off of him. While he is still making sure he has all the money to walk out Malcolm wakes up and pulls some string cheese out of his front pocket. Ricquo pauses for a second and looks at the audience

RICQUO

It's cheese man! Can ya blame me?

Ricquo walks off scene with the bag of money in hand. He returns a few moments later with no bag after outing it in the car and begins to sneak up on a sleeping Malcolm. Right when he is behind Malcolm Wade runs in and pulls Ricquo shoulder.

WADE

What the hell are you doing?! We got it. Let's get the hell outta here.

RICQUO

It's the cheese...He doesn't need it. I'm doing him a favor. Think of it like a good deed.

WADE

If he wakes up we're fucked. Let's get the hell outta here.

> At that moment Malcolm wakes up abruptly waving his walking stick in the air.

MALCOLM

Who the hell is there?! I smell a rat...and cheap cologne.

> Both Wade and Ricquo hide behind a desk while Malcom searches the bank for intruders.

MALCOLM

Bank's locked so you got nowhere to go now. Come out and show yourself. I'm armed and dangerous!

WADE

(Yelling but still trying to whisper)

God damnit...damnit damnit damnit. Over some fucking cheese?!

RICQUO

Stop crying we can still get outta here. I got an idea.

WADE

An idea? Let's get the fuck outta here. That's my idea.

RICQUO

Just follow my lead

WADE

"Just follow my lead" he said….alright fuck it. Your turn Einstein. Get us out of this one.

> Ricquo pauses a second to collect his words then goes over to Malcolm and taps him on the shoulder.

RICQUO

Excuse me sir! Can you help us find or way out of here.

> Malcolm turns around abruptly and immediately puts his fist up in a karate/fighting stance.

MALCOLM

You ain't going anywhere. The hell you doing in this bank after hours? We're closed.

RICQUO

Closed? Ahhh that's what that sign meant. The door must've been left open. I'm sorry for the confusion. I came to find my friend who has what one might call serious vision problems and has been sitting here for a while thinking it's a bus stop.

MALCOLM

I knew I could smell some cheap cologne...and rats.

RICQUO

Oh the smell....excuse me I'm a veterinarian. I just finished up surgery on some mice that had a few broken bones at our clinic.

MALCOLM

Surgery on a mouse? Now ain't that a waste of money...coulda just ate em. They taste delicious fried.

RICQUO

You sick son of a//

Wade nudges Ricquo hoping to get him back on track about getting the heck out of the bank.

WADE

Where the hell is the bus? I need to get home.

> Malcolm finally notices Wade, grabs his flashlight and puts the light uncomfortably close to Wade and Ricquo's eyes.

MALCOLM

(To Wade)

You smell like alcohol? You been drinking?

RICQUO

You smell like a heart attack//

WADE

(Under his breath to Ricquo)

Shut up...please shut up.

RICQUO

I'm sorry but what's up with the abnormally bright light in my face? Is that necessary?

MALCOLM

Look here boy...I ask the questions 'round here.

Malcolm slowly walks around the two as they stand there.

MALCOLM

You say your friend here is blind huh?

RICQUO

Yes sir. After he lost his eyesight he kinda started drinking every day to numb the pain. Looking at how alert you are I don't know if you've ever lost any your or had family who have but it could do a lot to you mentally. That's kinda why he drinks so much.

MALCOLM

Know anything about it?

> Malcolm takes off his sunglasses to show two eye patches covering both eyes.

MALCOLM

I know a lot about it. It all happened that one fateful day.

> Malcolm lowers the flashlight and begins to walk away from Wade and Ricquo to face the audience. The lights dim and a spotlight focus in on Malcolm as he tells his story.

MALCOLM

My whole life I've been the athletic outdoorsy type if ya couldn't tell.

> After he says this he takes a pull from his inhaler. While Malcolm is giving this monologue scene

changes to the exact situation Malcolm is talking about.

MALCOLM

I was ready to conquer the world. Till well...till it happened...After a hard workout back when I was a personal trainer I decided to treat myself to something to eat. As you can probably tell I'm a vegetarian and don't usually eat fast food. It was Friday so I was like "fuck it...it's the end of the week". Well I went to McDonalds and got the leanest cleanest healthiest things on the menu. Two Quarter Pounders...3 big macs...Four chicken sandwiches...a strawberry shake...Oh and a large fry. Yeah I remember that large fry. As I'm walking back to my house with my meal in hand I hear screaming. I run over to see her outside her burning house. She's screaming for someone to save her baby that's still indoors. First thing I'm thinking is "Bitch why didn't you grab your kid if you knew there was a fire?", but with the desire I've had since a little boy to be a superhero I dash inside the house without a second thought. Run through the burning cedar and grab the child in the cradle. I make it out the house covered in soot and that's when it happened.

RICQUO

Some of the fire got into your eyes?

MALCOLM

Huh? No I made it out safely then I went home and ate the McDonalds and got some sweet and sour sauce in my eyes then went blind. Just doesn't sound as cool if I leave the rest of the day out.

WADE

This guy here.

> MALCOLM

Hey don't you smart mouth me boy. I'm an American hero.

> RICQUO

I apologize sir. Didn't mean any disrespect. I mean you look like an American hero.

> MALCOLM

I know I know. Just use my skills now to protect those who can't protect themselves.

> RICQUO

Understandable sir.

Malcolm takes a sniff of Ricquo. Walks around him and takes a sniff again. Walks back around and takes another sniff.

> MALCOLM

You...you smell like blue cheese and baby oil. The same baby oil of that shat slut teller. Where you coming from boy?

Malcolm puts a flashlight directly in Ricquo's face. Ricquo doesn't know how to answer the question. He pauses for a bit.

RICQUO

Oh shit is that two immigrants outside burning the American flag?

MALCOLM

What the...I ain't letting nobody disrespect America like that!

Malcolm runs outside in attempt to find the burning flag.

RICQUO

(To wade)

When all else fails just throw America out there.

WADE

Let's get the fuck outta here.

Wade and Ricquo run out of the bank as quickly as possible. Scene goes to Ricquo and Wade are riding in the car. Adrenaline still pumping from their last encounter.

WADE

Whooo! We did it! We fuckin did it!

RICQUO

Ah man that was fun. Let's do it again. I wanna do it again!

WADE

We got the cash!

> In midst of their celebration wade searches his pockets for a cigarette.

I definitely need a smoke after that.

> Ricquo notices him looking and hands Wade a cigarette of his own.

WADE

Thanks.

> Wade lights the cigarette and pauses for a second.

Hey so what was he talking about back there about you and Julia?

RICQUO

Huh?

WADE

I said what was that security guard saying about you and Julia.

> Obviously lying, ricquo begins making up excuses and stumbling over his words.

RICQUO

Huh...Oh nothing. He thought we smelled the same.

> That answer sufficed enough for Wade so he didn't prod anymore.

WADE

Oh....I thought he was saying ya'll slept together or something

> Riqcuo lets out a chuckle that would basically say "Could you believe that?"

RICQUO

Oh wow...Ha never. I wish.

WADE

Yeah honestly me too. She looks pretty cute. I bet she has a nice ass spread.

RICQUO

(Under his breath)

Oh yeah she definitely does.

WADE

What ya say bro?

RICQUO

Oh I said yeah I bet. I need to see my cuz...cousin.

Completely unaware of Ricquo's remarks Wade smiles at Ricquo turns up the volume in the car and starts bobbing his head.

WADE

We're fuckin rich.

He puts his hand out I hopes of getting a fist bump. For the first time Ricquo fists bumps him back and they continue to bob their heads to the music. Scenes changes to back at Isaac's apartment, Isaac is lighting candles and trying to pick up stuff hoping to clean the place before Julia arrives. In the middle of running around and picking up the

> apartment, a knock on the door can be heard. Isaac anticipating Julia hurries to the door and opens it up. Julia walks in and they share a hug.

ISAAC

Hey, I 've missed you. I know we're not supposed to get attached and all but I enjoy seeing you twice in a day. Today must be special.

> Isaac tries to kiss Julia and she dodges his face. She walks past him and sits on the couch.

JULIA

How's your day been?

ISAAC

Not too bad..longer than expected.

JULIA

Yeah tell me about it.

ISAAC

I'm just glad I'm here with you so I can't say its too bad.

> Isaac sits on the couch and tries to put his arms

                                    around Julia.
                                    She stops him.

                JULIA

Hey I'm sorry but we need to talk.

                ISAAC

Ok...that works for me.

                                    Isaac puts his drink on
                                    the table sits back in
                                    the couch and turns to
                                    Julia

What's up?

                JULIA

I know we've been fooling around for a while now and I feel like there's something there//

                ISAAC

Me too

                JULIA

Let me finish...I don't know what this is....But I have to tell you that I think I'm in love.

                ISAAC

Oh my god...I've been thinking the same thing. You've been on my mind crazy lately...your just so special to me//

JULIA

No not with you...with someone else.

ISAAC

The fuck?

JULIA

I think I'm in love...and I had to let you know because I want to get serious with this guy. He's everything I've wanted in a man for a while.

                                  Isaac gets up from the couch and stands up scratching his head

ISAAC

I'm sorry...you lost me back there.

JULIA

Please...I thought I should be as honest with you as possible//

ISAAC

Somebody else? What about us?

JULIA

Hey love isn't planned...it just sorta happens.

ISAAC

You can't be serious.... Why are you telling me this?

JULIA

I am. When you find real love. You'll know. This guy is strong...sensitive...knows what he wants out of life. Great in bed. Honestly, I think I love him and I want to see where it goes.

ISAAC

So where does that leave us?

JULIA

Friends..we can still be friends.

ISAAC

Get the fuck outta my hosue

JULIA

I would but I'm waiting for my guy to come back and tell him how I feel. He still doesn't know.

ISAAC

Go wait at his house. Get the fuck out of here.

JULIA

Well see that's the thing. He lives here.

> At that moment Ricquo and Wade come bursting in filled with joy and adrenaline from the robbery.

WADE

(To Isaac)

We did it!

>Wade looks over towards Julia

Uhhh....What is she doing here?

ISAAC

I have no idea.

>Looking at Julia

Did you hit your head earlier or something?

>Julia runs over to Ricquo and embraces him.

JULIA

Hey baby. I've been thinking about you a lot since earlier.

ISAAC

What the fuck? Please don't tell me. Ricquo?

>Ricquo looks side to side multiple times hoping to avoid conflict.

RICQUO

Uhhh...I think I left my stuff downstairs. I'll be back.

>Ricquo begins to try and make his way to

>   the door but is stopped
>   by Isaac's voice.

                    ISAAC

RICQUO! What the hell is going on? Somebody please help me out.

>   Ricquo starts talking
>   very quietly to the
>   point where it sounds
>   like he's mumbling

                    RICQUO

            (Mumbling and fast)

See it kinda happened really fast. She came over then this sexual predator knocked on the door and I was alone and we had cheese and some wine and before you know it….

                    ISAAC

Speak up I can't even hear you.

>   A long pause while
>   Ricquo continues his
>   story.

                    RICQUO

    (Even lower than his current tone of voice)

I fucked Julia.

                    WADE

What?

                              RICQUO

I fucked Julia

                              ISAAC

What?

                              WADE

How?

                              RICQUO

I said I fucked Julia. Damn do I have to draw a picture along with it?

                                        Julia walks over to
                                        Ricquo to caress him.

No we made love.

                                        Ricquo gets free of her

                              RICQUO

 Bitch you tossed my salad while I sniffed cheese of your chest. That ain't love.

                              WADE

Whoa...she ate your salad? I still haven't got that off my bucket list.

                              ISAAC

How could you do that?

                              WADE

Well first you squat over her face. Preferably after a shower//

ISAAC

Shut the fuck up wade.

RICQUO

Look man. I'm sorry. It kinda just happened. It's nothing serious.

JULIA

What we shared isn't serious to you? I thought we had something special.

RICQUO

Bitch....I met you two days ago.

JULIA

Love doesn't have a timeframe. You know that.

ISAAC

Julia...wade could you guys leave is for a bit.

WADE

Sure

>   Wade and Julia make their way towards the door leaving Ricquo and Isaac in the apartment by themselves.

RICQUO

Look mann if you feel the need to hit me I'd understand-

>   Isaac closes in on
>   Ricquo and punches
>   Ricquo in the face.

I didn't mean actually hit me!

>   Ricquo avoids getting
>   close to Isaac. He keeps
>   his distance around the
>   couch.

                              RICQUO

I'm 14 pounds!...that qualifies as animal abuse.

>   They both keep going
>   around the couch. Isaac
>   trying to get closer to
>   Ricquo. Ricquo trying to
>   get farther away from
>   Isaac.

                              ISAAC

You knew I liked her.

                              RICQUO

If I would've known this much I swear I wouldn't have. It kinda just happened.

                              ISAAC

Just happened?

                              RICQUO

Yeah just happened.

ISAAC

We left the house..you saw her leave..you saw me this morning with her?//

RICQUO

First off...Why the hell are you mad at me?

ISAAC

I liked her//

RICQUO

You sound like a bitch....fuck...this just shows you you liked the wrong one

> Long silence while Ricquo and Isaac stand there separated by the couch in between them

RICQUO

Look man...I'm sorry. A little bit of cheese and wine led to one thing or the other.

> Isaac walks away from the couch to the kitchen grabs a beer and sits on the couch. Ricquo pops up behind the couch still a bit timid to sit down in

> hopes to avoid further physical contact from Isaac. Wade comes into the apartment.

                              WADE

Hey um I'm sorry to interrupt but have any of you guys seen my wallet?

> Isaac glares at him not wanting to give him an answer. Wade slowly steps back out the apartment. Long silence while Isaac drinks a beer and Ricquo is still behind the couch.

                              ISAAC

I think you should move out//

                             RICQUO

C'mon man...over a bitch? If that's what you want I know some slots....three mice that'll lick your balls from behind//

                              ISAAC

It ain't even about Julia...It's the..I don't know man.

> Isaac chugs the rest of the beer and puts his jacket on in

> preparation to leave. He walks out while Ricquo is still talking to him.

                    RICQUO

Hey don't worry about the bong man!

> Scene changes to Isaac walking down the street. Isaac stops under a street light to light a cigarette. Smokes a couple puffs and coughs then throws it away. He keeps walking. Isaac crosses the street and walks toward a coffee shop. When he opens the door, Isaac literally bumps into Clarissa at a coffee shop while he's entering and she's leaving. She drops her coffee.

                    ISAAC

Oh my...I am so so sorry

                    CLARISSA

No no it's fine

> Isaac looks up for a second while picking up the spilled drinks

ISAAC

Clarissa?

She looks up as well

CLARISSA

(Obviously flustered and awkwardly)

Hey !

They embrace for a hug.

ISAAC

How's everything been? It's been forever since I've seen you...how's everything been?

CLARISSA

I've been good. Can't complain about too much. How about you?

ISAAC

I've been better but I'm breathing so...yeah what's up? Let me buy you another coffee. That's the least I can do since I dropped your all over the floor.

CLARISSA

It's fine...I may just be a sign that I need to stay away from coffee//

ISAAC

Please...it's the least I can do.

> Clarissa hesitates before answering

CLARISSA

Ok. I'll take you up on the offer.

> Isaac and Clarissa walk back into the coffee shop. Isaac goes up to the counter.

ISAAC

One caramel macchiato and?-

CLARISSA

Um a Captain crunch Frappuccino please

ISAAC

One caramel macchiato and one Captain Crunch Frappuccino

CASHIER

The total will be 11.65

> Isaac reaches down in to his pocket and gives the cashier a 20. The cashier rings it up and gives Isaac his change.

ISAAC

Thank you.

> Isaac puts his change back in his pocket.

ISAAC

Shall we take a seat while we wait?

CLARISSA

Sure.

Isaac leads the way to a table. He pulls out the chair for Clarissa.

CLARISSA

Thank you.

Isaac sits down as well.

ISAAC

How have you been? You look great.

CLARISSA

I've been ok. Juggling work with my personal life has been my main priority.

ISAAC

Where do you work at?

CLARISSA

Um I work at...this financial firm place. Just pushing papers you know.

ISAAC

Oh ok. That's cool.

CLARISSA

What about you? How've you been? Last time I talked to you was after your graduation. I remember you kept talking about law school

ISAAC

I've...let's say I had to put that on hold for a bit.

CLARISSA

Understandable...Life kinda makes you do that sometimes.

>Isaac looks Clarissa in the eye

ISAAC

Honestly I don't know.

CLARISSA

That's pretty honest.

ISAAC

Yeah....so many people ask that question with no true desire to find out how someone's really doing and so many people answer just to keep up appearances but honestly I can say I've had better days.

CLARISSA

We all have...they get better.

ISAAC

I remember when I met you sophomore year in the dorms....I threw up in your car the first day I met you.

CLARISSA

And I had to take care of you that night...you were too too wasted.

>Isaac and Clarissa laugh
>about that memory

ISAAC

I remember when it happened I was so embarrassed about it but ever since then I was kinda glad that I did.

CLARISSA

Why?

ISAAC

Well I never would've got to meet you...

>Cashier puts their
>drinks on the counter

ISAAC

Oh they're ready...

>Isaac gets up and goes
>to the counter to grab
>the drinks. Isaac comes
>back to the table and
>hands Clarissa hers.

CLARISSA

Thank You.

>They both take a sip.

ISAAC

I never tried that before how is it?

CLARISSA

Kinda became my favorite drink here…try it.

> Clarissa hands him the drink. In the exchange their hands touch for a moment.

ISAAC

That's pretty damn good…I could see how you could get addicted to it.

CLARISSA

Now you see the dilemma…to quit Starbucks or to not quit Starbucks. My life is Hamlet's.

ISAAC

Do what makes you feel good…

CLARISSA

That's a dilemma in itself

ISAAC

Eh….

> They both sit silently for a second drinking coffee and looking at each other.

ISAAC

I'm fine.

CLARISSA

What?

ISAAC

I'm fine...I mean you asked me earlier how I'm doing and right now the answer would be I'm fine.

CLARISSA

I'm glad to hear. What changed for you?

ISAAC

Running into you...literally. I mean this moment...It makes me feel fine. I learned a lot opening the door to starbucks today. Who woulda thought?

CLARISSA

What did you learn?

ISAAC

A lot about myself and what I want.

CLARISSA

What did you learn about yourself?

ISAAC

I can't try to fill holes in my life with Band-Aids.

CLARISSA

What?

ISAAC

It's a long story.

CLARISSA

We got half a drink left. Give me a summary.

ISAAC

Kinda thought I liked this girl. I was trying to force something that honestly I knew wasn't there.

CLARISSA

I see

ISAAC

Yeah me too. Finally took off the Ray Charles glasses.

CLARISSA

God for you.

ISAAC

Thanks..........Ever since we kinda fell through I been trying to replace you in the nicest way possible I meant that but what I mean is that for me..well I just gotta wait for someone who comes across and that feeling is really genuine.

                        Clarissa looks Isaac in the eyes.

ISAAC

I'm not saying I want a relationship or anything like that. I loved you and still do. I know that what we had now isn't something I can just replace.

> Clarissa's phone rings. She looks down at the text and looks back up at Isaac

CLARISSA

Yeah it's a lonely feeling thinking you're in it by yourself. I've been there myself.

ISAAC

Do you still think about us?

CLARISSA

Of course.

ISAAC

I think about us a lot...what could've been...what was...what isn't.

CLARISSA

Yeah a lot of time passes by when you're sitting there thinking though.

ISAAC

Tis' true

CLARISSA

I'm sorry to cut this short but I gotta go.

ISAAC

Oh going to work?

CLARISSA

No I'm going to go pick up my daughter. She's at the baby sitter.

ISAAC

You have a child? Oh my...Congratulations

CLARISSA

Thank you

ISAAC

What's her name?

CLARISSA

Alana

ISAAC

I love that name.

ISAAC

She's definitely a jewel. As beautiful as her mother I know already.

Clarissa smiles at Isaac

ISAAC

How old is she?

CLARISSA

She's almost 2...

ISAAC

Terrible two- Wait we were dating two years ago.

CLARISSA

I know

Isaac sits back in his seat and looks at Clarissa

ISAAC

Babies aren't made by themselves//

CLARISSA

She's yours....I just didn't want or think I needed to tell you when I found out. Thought where we were it was best we just went our separate ways. Look I got to go//

ISAAC

You can't just leave after telling me something like that. I have a daughter?

CLARISSA

I promise you don't have to worry about//

ISAAC

I want worry about it...that's my daughter.

> Clarissa pauses for a second

CLARISSA

Let's talk about this later

> Clarissa writes her number on a napkin and hands it to Isaac

CLARISSA

It was great catching up and give this to your friend.

> Clarissa leaves leaving Isaac with Wade's wallet and a napkin with her number on it on the table. Isaac sees it only has 5 numbers on it.

END OF PLAY

V.   Distinction between Consciousness and Ego

I can say and with the utmost honestly and insecurity, I have no idea who I am. I have blindly subjected myself for 25 years to the unfounded social and cultural convictions of others. Cultural and social narratives have painted pictures for me of who I'm supposed to be, but the mask I have to wear is uncomfortable enough that I know it is simply that, a mask.

William Wordsworth once said "The child is the father of the man". I'm yet to comprehend it. Unable still to formulate a response in a cohesive manner that is eloquent enough to convey, but I can feel it. This essay isn't merely to inform or for dialogue, but quite honestly just an escape from my individual hell of reason. Being cognizant of the distinction between consciousness and ego is something that has occupied me for a while. To further discuss the topic I need to define the ideas I associate with ego and consciousness, respectively. In my understanding, the ego is not a congealed, heteronymous object, but rather a fluid, autonomous subject. Also in its very origins, a repository for the projected desires and fantasies of larger others; the child's image is a receptacle for his/her parents dreams and wishes, with his/her body image being always already overwritten by signifiers flowing from the libidinal economies of other speaking beings. Hence, recognizing the ego as "me", as embodying and representing an authentic, private, unique selfhood that is most genuinely my own, is tantamount to misrecognizing that, at root, the ego is ultimately an alienating foreign introject through which I am seduced and subjected by others conscious and unconscious wants and machinations. Ultimately, the ego is something "extimate" (i.e., intimately exterior, an internal externality) insofar as it crystallizes "the desire of the other".

The idea of the other is one of the primary issues that stem from recognizing the ego as a primary existence, within this dynamic the master/ slave dialect arises. The master-slave dialect is an idea whereas two "egos" come in contact and are astounded at the realization of the self as a foreign object. This forms what we would refer to as self consciousness. While both parties can choose to ignore the other party and let them become an animate part of the experience, it's nearly if not utterly impossible, because innately we seek for affirmation of our own existence through others. Though this doesn't happen initially, it is an end result of the relationship. Initially, we are mesmerized by the mirror like other and attempt, as we previously had before coming into contact to assert our will. Struggle ensues, however both parties are subconsciously aware that they are dependent on the existence of the other. An agreement is therefore implemented, where death is avoided by subordination to "slavery".

For the sake of the reader, I am using the term slavery loosely to identify with numerous definitions. This creates friction between the two parties. According to Hegel, "On approaching the other it has lost its own self, since it finds itself as another being; secondly, it has thereby sublated that other, for this primitive consciousness does not regard the other as essentially real but sees its own self in the other". I don't know if there's anything to counter being seductively overcome by the identity of the ego outside of being cognizant of it.

Lacan proposed what he coined as the "Mirror Stage Theory". The mirror stage theory supposes that ego arises as early as 2 years old. Once the subject recognizes the image in the mirror as self, the child begins to look at other adult beings similar to itself as omnipotent. This stems from the child being wholly dependent on the adults for survival. Through development, the child begins to project an ideal self emulating what traits and characteristics he deems necessary to reach the level of the omnipotent beings it once depended on for survival.

Unaware of the developing ego, the child begins to identify the ego as "me". Every individual at some point in their life or throughout their whole lives face this battle unknowingly in conflict and strife, due to the acknowledgement of the ego as self. The irony lies in the arbitrary meaning we put on the beliefs of others rather than defining our own existence. The social apparatus has paved the way for individuals to find affirmation in their employment/class status.

Within the realm of the ego strife is always prevalent and arises when desires seductively promise the feeling of happiness, fulfillment, or affirmation but they never deliver. Consciousness is a more abstract definition to grasp. Painted by ideas and language, the way an artist would put a brush to a canvas it's understood as an omnipresent awareness. It is the feeling of what has happened, what is happening, and what could happen within the body and our environment. Consciousness gives us the ability to escape from the here and now of linear time. My understanding of consciousness has I believed been discussed under many names and flags of identity. From the term "Akasha", which is a Sanskrit term that in English means "sky" or "aether", to the names of breathe, life, or "will" according to Schopenhauer, and even as recently as the Zero Point Field, for me it rings the same idea. For a more concise understanding I hope, I will refer to consciousness as the "ZPF" or Zero Point Field.

In physics, the Zero Point Field is a consequence of something long known to particle physicists known as the Heisenberg Uncertainty Principle. It states that if we know the position of a sub-atomic particle we cannot know its speed, and if we know its speed we cannot know its momentum. If a particle were at rest, then we would know both. One truth we do know is that particles stays in motion, even at the coldest state known in science which is minus 273.15 degrees Celsius.

Reasonably speaking, there should be no energy at absolute zero, but there is. All space is filled with this energy. It fills everything and changes what we think is a vacuum into a space that is absolutely filled to the brim with energy, technically known as "Plenum". This is an interesting parallel with ancient philosophy that there is no such thing as empty space. Chang Tsai believed the bedrock of reality was the "Ch'i" which translates into either gas or ether. He believed it was a tenuous and non-perceptible form of matter which is present throughout space and can condense into solid material objects. The idea that matter somehow condenses out of the "Ch'I" is amazingly prescient because this is a process that echoes the most ancient of ideas.

Indian physicist Satyendra Nath Bose was a scientist brought up within eastern ideologies rather than the philosophical western tradition. He believed that if particles were cooled to a few degrees above absolute zero they may change from being a single particle to a collection of particles that act is if they were one. In principle, all the particles within the condensate have become one, a single particle spread out in space-time. The condensates pull their energy out of the Zero Point Field in the form of Zero Point Energy. Many of us put this theory in practice, when we listen to a CD player or use a DVD player, i.e. the information from the disc is read using a laser beam and a laser beam is technically coherent light (a beam in which all the light particles 'photons' are all sharing a single coherent state).

Another application of this theory deals primarily with the human brain. What we take to be an external reality is a construct of the brain modeled out of the electro-chemical information supplied to it from our senses. Holograms are three dimensional images created by using lasers to "photograph" an object and then reproduce the subsequent image by illuminating it with another set of lasers. This again is an application of coherent light, in which a seemingly a seemingly solid image can be reproduced from stored information. In 1986, two Japanese researchers, Isuki Hirano and Atsushi Hirai suggested that coherent light is generated in vast quantities by tiny structures in the brain called microtubules. These microtubules are so small that is may be possible that the energy they use to generate coherent light is Zero Point Energy from the ZPF of Zero Point Field. If we are to move forward with the supposition, then it is safe to say the brain has direct access to the Zero Point Field.

Again, I stress this is simply an opinion of mine just like any other theory which we structure our lives around. For me the distinction of consciousness and ego is a dilemma which we have to address in order to move forward. The fundamental delusion of our contemporary perception is the dogma that I am here and you are out there. The paradigm of our world one could suppose limits our ability to encounter vitality in daily life. Hypothetically speaking, the general consciousness of social individuals focuses only on the act of rowing the boat and those events that are related to rowing such as directions, efforts, and goals. Such a consciousness is limited in the sense that it is primarily aware of only the boat, the oars, and their activity. Such an individual mistakes these elements for an actual location and measure of connection with the world around them. They become divided and only relate to the world insofar as it is related to their perceived short-term goals. Every failure to cope with a life situation must be laid, in the end, to a restriction of consciousness. Wars and temper tantrums are the makeshifts of ignorance. The individual has only to discover his own position with reference to this general human formula and let it then assist him past his restricting walls.

VI. Constraints of Language

In order to think outside the box, we must eliminate the box we put ourselves in. Fillippo Marinetti once said "Time and space died yesterday". What I grasped from this quote is that human evolution is yielded or not able to reach its full potential due to our constant grasp on beliefs from past generations. We're trapped in linguistic constructs. As humans, we reason about reality through the lenses of categories. Categories are expressed linguistically through words. I perceive language to be a subjective agreement by a group of people to conceptualize and verbalize their interpretation of reality. Language is a decoding process for human consciousness. It also is one of the most effective ways to express ideas between individuals and to ourselves. The social agreement (language) allows people to understand and implement ideas. We also overlap our language onto nature, in order to understand the workings of the world. Our senses allow us to perceive reality, and through language we give meanings, titles and names to these particular experiences.

Unfortunately, through the use of language we unintentionally create stoppage with words. Everything is constantly moving, and even in a new structure it is still and always the original form. There is no such thing as past, present or future. It just is. For me, the idea that language is created inside one's mind independently of outside experiences eliminates the possibility that the external world is the common source of all language. Therefore, each language creates its own reality. For example, a wooden table comes from a tree but we refer to its current form as a table. Is it not still a tree? In 1,000,000 years the same energy that was a table will take a different form. As people believe in contemporary circles, nothing is created or destroyed. The language we use hampers us into the present. Unknowingly, we buy into the idea of "Presentism". We have disillusioned the original forms in motion and bought into a stagnant reality. Nouns as we know them have the tendency to imply static, creating a state of stoppage such as that of a linear experience. Recognition of the human condition which is constantly in flux, creates a paradigm where you can understand the idea of life being a continuous experience with series of transitions.

Time is another apriori notion that consciousness has developed, which I see as a barrier. Time is a concept we attach to events happening within in a particular space. An event in space/time is a particular point in a cosmological space at a particular moment. Time and space are intertwined via coordinates in order to describe bodies in movement. Language and time have fallen from their absolute statues. Even though they create the dimensional framework of our current reality, they both are sustained on inadvertent false perception.

www.ingramcontent.com/pod-product-compliance
Lightning Source LLC
LaVergne TN
LVHW051119080426
835510LV00018B/2131